POSTCARD HISTORY S

Early Chicago Hotels

On the front cover: **AUDITORIUM HOTEL, LOBBY.** Designed by Dankmar Adler and Louis Sullivan and built between 1886 and 1890, the Auditorium building was the largest building in America. It contained a 400-room hotel, an office and retail space, and the world's most acoustically perfect theater. The lobby shows Sullivan at his best with his signature doorway and stairwell arches detailed with botanic tracery and intricate Roman mosaic floor. This view from the elevator lobby features the grand staircase and front office. (EA.)

On the back cover: **SOUTH HYDE PARK BOULEVARD, SHOWING COOPER-CARLTON AND SISSON HOTELS.** The Sisson Hotel (left), built in 1917, and the Cooper-Carlton (right), constructed in 1918, were both designed in the Classical Revival style by the architectural firm of Newhouse and Bernham and built in conjunction with and meant to complement one another. The hotels overlook a section of Burnham Park, now named for Chicago's first African American mayor, Harold Washington, who once lived at the Hampton House, formerly the Sisson. (GB.)

POSTCARD HISTORY SERIES

Early Chicago Hotels

William R. Host and Brooke Ahne Portmann

ISBN 0-7385-4041-2

Published by Arcadia Publishing
Charleston SC, Chicago IL, Portsmouth NH, San Francisco CA

Printed in the United States of America

Library of Congress Catalog Card Number: 2006923699

For all general information contact Arcadia Publishing at:
Telephone 843-853-2070
Fax 843-853-0044
E-mail sales@arcadiapublishing.com
For customer service and orders:
Toll-Free 1-888-313-2665

Visit us on the Internet at http://www.arcadiapublishing.com

To my parents, Bill and Dorothy, who taught me to always set an extra place at the table, and to my life partner, Denis Frankenfield, for his nourishment of both the body and the soul.
— WRH

To my parents, Bonnie and Frank, from whom I learned the transformative power of gracious hospitality, the value of family dinners with candlelight, and the pleasures of quiet hotels, and to Paul, for tall pine trees, snow angels at midnight, and page 282.
— BAP

Contents

ACKNOWLEDGMENTS

This book grew from our shared passions for both hospitality and the arts. It has become a reality because of the support and goodwill of a great many people and institutions.

We extend special thanks to the research librarians at the Chicago History Museum and the staffs at the Chicago Public Library, Newberry Library, Regenstein Library of the University of Chicago, Roosevelt University archives, the Art Institute of Chicago, and the Hyde Park Historical Society. Special thanks to Richard Joncas, Harrington College of Design, for sharing his passion for interior design and its history; and to Robert V. Allegrini, the Hilton Chicago; and Ken Price, Palmer House Hilton, for sharing their resources, expertise, and fascination for the grand hotels of Chicago. We express our gratitude to American Institute of Architects-Chicago Chapter's Alice Sinkevitch and Joan Pomeranc for their vast knowledge, advice, and encouragement in this project. We are grateful to our readers Arny Reichler, Deborah Perry, Valerie Gager, and Greg Maravolo for providing counsel especially when we wondered if anyone else would find what we had uncovered engaging. For their inspiration, we thank fellow Arcadia authors Leslie Hudson and David Stone.

We thank our colleagues, faculty, and staff at Roosevelt University's Evelyn T. Stone University College, and Roosevelt University for Brooke's research leave.

Our college professors instilled in us a passionate obsession for the arts; for this, we honor Jack Banta, Art History, Kutztown University of Pennsylvania (Kutztown State College); and Roland Flint, English, Georgetown University. Their legacy lives beyond them.

We could not have done this without the support, confidence, and interest of our good friends, brothers, and sister. And finally, thanks to Lea, Sam, and Taj for keeping us honest.

OLD KINZIE HOUSE. It was the first house built in Chicago. (VOH.)

Introduction

While its landscape offered little physical beauty and its air revealed the source of its name *Chicagou* or "place of the wild onion or skunkweed," Chicago was valued by the American Indians and early European traders because of its strategic location at the intersection of a great lake, the prairies, and a network of rivers. The first non-native resident, Jean Baptiste DuSable, arrived in the early 1790s and built a home and trading post at the mouth of the Chicago River, where he lived until the early 1800s. To protect the land and traders, the American government established Fort Dearborn near DuSable's home. Chicago incorporated as a town in 1833, with a population of 100 and received its city charter in 1837.

During the years between 1830 and 1871, Chicago's population burgeoned from 100 to over 300,000 residents. Ambitious urban pioneers established slaughterhouses, breweries, lumber mills, shipyards, steel mills, printing houses, and granaries. The city was linked to the East and West Coasts by water, stagecoach, and telegraphic communications. By 1860, railroad lines transformed Chicago into the nation's transportation hub and charted the city's path to becoming the country's business center and the site for political, social, and trade conventions. But Chicagoans desired more than industry and money. By 1867, the city had three colleges, a school of music, public schools, an opera company, an orchestra, and several theaters. And it had hotels.

The hotel, a freestanding, specially built structure with diverse services for travelers and local citizens, was an American invention. Most travelers in the colonies and early republic lodged at taverns and inns that were indistinguishable from homes. Created to meet the needs of travelers and city residents, the nation's first hotels gradually advanced standards and amenities: Washington, D.C.'s, Union Hotel (1793) provided meeting rooms on the first floor and lodging on the second; the City Hotel in New York (1794) added private bedrooms; and Boston's Coffee House Exchange (1808) included ballrooms, public reading rooms, an atrium, an observatory, and stores for travelers and city residents.

To encourage citizens to patronize the new hotels, city leaders, financial backers, and hoteliers furnished the lobbies and parlors as elegantly as the homes of the wealthy to create a sense of the familiar. Use of the word "*hotel*," French for "a private residence," reinforced the elegance and exclusivity of these stylish venues. Occasionally naming the local accommodations "house" conveyed a sense of safety and hospitality in contrast to the perceived unsavory character of an inn or tavern.

From the late 18th century onward, cities that could boast a hotel, and not a mere flea-infested tavern, had demonstrated both their prosperity and their forward-looking gaze. Hotels were not only expressions of generosity and welcome, but also harbingers of commerce, capitalism, and competition.

Chicago and other frontier cities repeated the East Coast pattern of public hospitality development—from inns and taverns to hotels, albeit at a much faster rate. From their rise in the 1830s, Chicago's hotels were bustling centers of city life. Out-of-town guests and local citizens gathered there to wheel and deal in business, climb the social ladder, engage in rough and tumble politics, and swoon at the newest inventions of modern life.

Chicago's Great Fire in October 1871 ended this rapid development when it destroyed its 28 downtown hotels in an area also comprising Chicago's most significant government, business, manufacturing, and commercial buildings.

While the fire marked the end of Chicago's initial development, it also gave birth to a new sense of luxury and technical achievement and provided an opportunity for improvements in construction. As a result of engineering advances over the next decade in fireproofing, utilization of the iron and steel frame, and innovations in stabilizing foundations, hotels expanded upward, soaring to 17 stories in 1890.

By the opening of the 1893 World's Columbian Exposition, Chicago had built between 1,400 and 2,000 hotels and lodging houses for the more than 27 million fair visitors. Catering largely to white wealthy, commercial, and middle classes, hotels met the needs of families and special-interest groups. They housed people on tours and attending conventions, honest sellers, and hucksters on the make. People flocked to hotels because they modeled new domestic interiors, promoted conspicuous consumption and display, and were showcases for the newest technology—hot and cold running water, telephones, electric lights, and air conditioning. These amenities and innovations established the early era of the modern hotel.

Hotel construction in Chicago occurred in three major periods between 1871 and World War I. The first was immediately following the fire. The second began during the late 1880s and lasted through 1893. No new hotels appeared during the nearly decade-long national depression following the exposition. But by the early 20th century, existing hotels began to renovate or add annexes, and new construction got underway (and remained strong until the Depression).

This book begins with a brief history of Chicago hotels from the city's first lodging in 1829 to the Great Fire of 1871. Chapter 2 discusses architectural and interior design styles while chapters 3 through 7 explore the hotels by location, and in chronological order of construction in the city—the Central Business District, the North Side, and the South Side with a focus on and Hyde Park. The book closes with a brief look at the hotels of the 1920s, ushering in the era of the grand hotel.

A listing of postcard sources and a brief bibliography are included on the final pages. The postcards in this book date from 1904 through the 1940s, covering five eras of postcard publishing. Private mailing cards (1898–1901) were printed by publishers other than the U.S. Government. Undivided-back era cards (1901–1907) limited writing to the small space on the image side and devoted the entire back to the address. Divided-back era cards (1907–1915), the golden age of postcards, permitted both message and address on one side and an image on the reverse. The white border card era lasted from 1916 through 1930. Finally linen era cards (1930–1945) were made from a linen-type paper stock using vivid colors.

One

Chicago Hotel History 1829-1871

In 1829, at the fork of the Chicago River close to where the river met Lake Michigan, traders and frontiersmen could find lodging at one of Chicago's three inns: Caldwell's Tavern, Miller's Tavern, and the Eagle Exchange (later called the Sauganash).

These did not last long. The Tremont House, the city's first freestanding hotel, was opened in 1833 at the corner of Lake and Dearborn Streets. Chicago's second hotel, the City Hotel, was built in 1837 and then expanded and renamed the Sherman House in 1845 by its new owner and Chicago mayor Francis C. Sherman. Railroads began to connect Chicago to the rest of the nation in 1848, and by 1853 the Sherman House was at a prime location, halfway between water and rail transportation.

Because Chicago was at the nation's transportation crossroads, the city became the meeting center as well. It hosted its first national meeting, the River and Harbor Convention in 1845, attracting as many as 20,000 people. From this success, Chicago went on to host Republican and Democratic national conventions, the National Ship-Canal Convention in 1863, and others. With the continued growth of transportation, commerce, manufacturing, and conventions, Chicago was seen as a major business hub of the nation.

However, on October 8, 1871, this progress was interrupted with what became known as the Great Fire. Continuing for 27 hours, it destroyed 3.5 square miles, killed an estimated 250, and left 90,000 homeless. Property losses exceeded $200 million, and the fire devastated 17,450 buildings. But the city was destroyed only temporarily. The fire stirred the passions of architects, builders, and financiers and gave the city the opportunity to begin with a fresh palette of architectural ideas.

CHICAGO IN 1832, WOLF'S POINT AT THE JUNCTION OF THE TWO BRANCHES OF THE CHICAGO RIVER. A flag flying above a building displays the image of a lone wolf, identifying this site as Wolf Point. The buildings are likely Chicago's first three inns: the Eagle Exchange (later called the Sauganash), Caldwell's Tavern, and Miller's Tavern. Sauganash proprietor, Mark Beaubien, held the first concerts here and provided space for Chicago's first theatrical performance.

LAKE HOUSE (1835–1871 FIRE), SOUTHEAST CORNER, RUSH AND HUBBARD STREETS. Built in 1835 and located where the Wrigley building sits today, Lake House became a political and social center. Soon other hotels, including the Briggs, the Richmond, and the Matteson Houses, were built, as were numerous smaller lodging houses near rail depots and the lakefront. Prior to the Great Fire of 1871, at least 30 hotels were located in Chicago's central business district. (Courtesy of the Chicago History Museum.)

TREMONT HOUSE (1850–1871 FIRE), SOUTHEAST CORNER, LAKE AND DEARBORN STREETS. After two earlier constructions burned to the ground, a third Tremont House, designed by Chicago's first architect John M. Van Osdel, emerged in 1850. The 260-room hotel was one of the most prominent in the city. Lincoln and Douglas began their senatorial campaigns with speeches from its balcony. In 1860, it served as headquarters for the Republican National Convention. (Courtesy of the Chicago History Museum.)

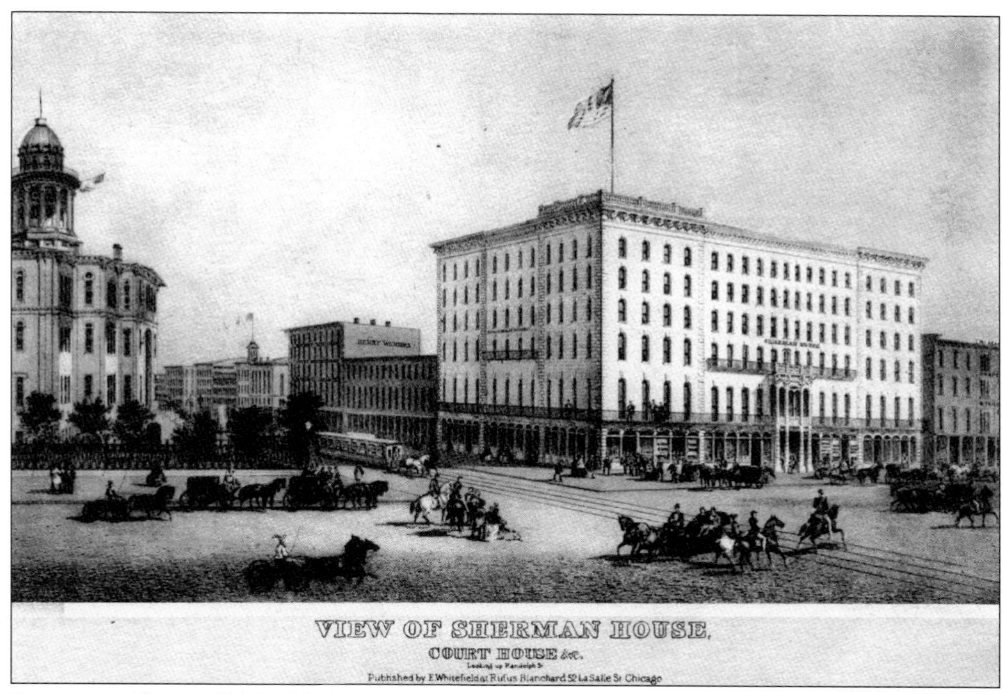

SHERMAN HOUSE (1861–1871 FIRE) AND COURT HOUSE SQUARE, NORTHWEST CORNER, RANDOLPH AND CLARK STREETS. Designed by W. W. Boyington between the lake and the river, the Sherman House was sited with the financial district on the southwest, the merchant district to the north, and city hall and the courthouse across the street. The six-story hotel attracted traders and financiers and became one of the city's premiere luxury hotels. (Courtesy of the Chicago History Museum.)

Grand Pacific Hotel and Embers of Chicago Fire (1871–1871). Both the new Grand Pacific Hotel and the new Palmer House were open only briefly before the fire. (Records on their openings differ anywhere from one day to 10 months prior to the fire.) Here a skeleton of charred ruins was all that remained of the Grand Pacific—a scene that became symbolic of Chicago's devastation. John Drake (Tremont House) and J. Irving Pearce (Sherman House) temporarily relocated their hotels. Other hoteliers started anew. Built from plans readily available, the Grand Pacific Hotel and the Palmer House were the first two new hotels after the fire. (Courtesy of the Chicago History Museum.)

Two

ARCHITECTURAL AND INTERIOR STYLES

At first, Chicago's engineers and architects borrowed from existing traditions. They created buildings and designed rooms based upon ideas from architecture and interior design developed in other times for people of other circumstances. Gradually, the city's architects began to work with and respond to the new materials and needs of people in this city, including both the people who paid for the construction of the buildings and those who would use them.

This chapter explores the architectural and interior design styles seen most often among the hotels in this book and identifies key features for those styles.

Neoclassical: Hotel Windermere. Classically inspired indicates a style can be traced to Greece and Rome. Concern for rectangularity is attributed to Greece and curvilinearity to Rome. Pediments, a triangular gable, are Greek, while domes are Roman. Columns used for support, like the two-story columns with Ionic capitals shown here (far left) are from the Greeks. Single-story columns and pilasters (decorative columns embedded in walls or door openings) are from the Romans. The Palladian window in the pediment at the left is from the Renaissance.

Italianate Style: Briggs House. The Italianate style (1840–1885) features tall, narrow windows and a flat roofline with an overhanging cornice supported by brackets. While the Briggs's windows are fairly plain, Italianate windows can be highly ornamental and may be arched, inverted U–shaped, or rectangular. Some Italianate structures may also have a tower. Other Italianate-style hotels include New Gault, Windsor-Clifton, Victoria, and Revere House. (1915.)

SECOND EMPIRE STYLE: STRATFORD HOUSE. The Second Empire style (1855–1885) comes from the French, recognizable for its mansard roof (roofing material covers the final story). Dormers may interrupt the roof, and some buildings have rectangular or square towers. Quoins (stonework, usually at corners) may appear. Molded cornices at the upper and lower roof edges are frequent, with decorative brackets under the lower cornice. Italianate and Second Empire styles feature similar window and door ornamentation. See Grand Pacific (1873), Palmer (1873), Sherman (1873), and Tremont. (WN, 1906.)

BEAUX ARTS STYLE: NEW WABASH HOTEL. Beaux Arts (1885–1930) buildings are classically inspired, but their surfaces are exuberantly decorated with garlands, floral patterns, or shields. Quoins, columns, and pilasters (columns embedded in walls) appear frequently, and cornices are elaborate. Roofs are either flat or mansard; first floors are often rusticated. Finials at the roofline and pointed arches (postcard) are in the medieval style. See Blackstone, La Salle, Sherman (1911), Sisson, and Cooper-Carlton. (CT, 1932.)

CHICAGO SCHOOL OR CHICAGO CONSTRUCTION: HOTEL WARNER. With 1880s advances in the iron and steel frame and innovations in stabilizing foundations, Chicago's architects developed a plain-styled building, erected quickly and at a lesser cost. Features include pressed brick exterior walls, rounded corners, and bay windows creating undulating, long side walls to infuse more light and air into interiors. Verticality is often emphasized. Ground floors are of rusticated stone. Hotels within this category include Hyde Park, Auditorium, Great Northern, Virginia, the Plaza, Metropole, Lexington, and Lakota.

TRIPARTITE: FORT DEARBORN HOTEL. Chicago architect Louis Sullivan argued that because "skyscrapers were essentially vertical in nature they should be designed as if they were a column with an articulated base, an uninterrupted shaft, and a capital on termination." This is tripartite theory and can be found in styles including Chicago construction, Beaux Arts, and Neoclassical. See Auditorium, Blackstone, Pearson, Sisson, Cooper-Carlton, and Stevens. (VOH, 1915.)

VICTORIAN: SARATOGA HOTEL, PARLOR BEDROOM. This style permeated the latter part of the 19th century though Queen Victoria's death in 1901. It can still be observed in many American hotel interiors in the 1900s. Victorians were driven by *horror vacui,* or fear of empty spaces, resulting in crowded arrangements of comfortably tufted furniture, heavily draped tables, and voluminous wall decor. They also preferred ferns, fringe, mystery, surprise, the exotic, and the colors of red and green. (CT.)

GENERIC CLASSICAL INTERIOR: STRATFORD HOTEL, ENTRANCE TO LOBBY. Classical features here include the decorative Doric columns, dentil (teeth-like) cornice just below the ceiling, geometric fret or Greek key along the edges of the floor, and the corridor's overall linearity and symmetry. The room is enhanced with favored elements of the era, including tall palm trees and stained-glass windows.

English Styles: the Blackstone, English Room. Manor houses of the English Restoration (1660–1702) featured wood-paneled walls and strapwork ceilings, including decorative pendants. Spool-and-knob legs and carved backs originated in the Elizabethan period (1558–1603), while spiral columns, turned legs, tall backs, and upholstery are from the Restoration period. Because light was needed, windows in manors were clear glass. The stained-glass windows, drapes, and chandeliers (postcard) are interpolations upon English elements. (ML.)

Baroque or Louis XIV-Style: the Blackstone, Ball and Banquet Room. Baroque began in late 16th century Italy. Reflecting Louis XIV's (1643–1715) concern for presentation, Louis XIV-style is considered French baroque. Gilding, cartouches or shield motifs, and stretchers connecting furniture legs were frequent. Designers coordinated furniture, walls, floors, and ceilings as a whole, or en suite, and carefully placed furniture at the edges of a room. While found in France, white rooms were prevalent in northern Europe. (ML.)

ROCOCO OR LOUIS XV-STYLE: HOTEL LA SALLE, THE GRAND BALL ROOM. Following the extreme concern for public presentation of Louis XIV, the pendulum turned under Louis XV (1714-1774) and a lighter sensibility developed. The chief characteristics of Louis XV-style or rococo are its curvilinearity, lightness, and delicateness. The term rococo is derived from the scallop shell or rocaille, one of the most frequent motifs seen on walls, furniture, and ceilings. Chair and table legs now curve, called cabriole, and are no longer held together by stretchers. This Grand Ball Room reflects additional key conventions of the style, including merging of walls and ceilings, and ceilings painted to give the illusion of a sky overhead. Continuing from the baroque, the architecture and furniture are designed as an ensemble, with a concern for comfort that resulted in new chair shapes (e.g., wingback, chaise lounge, and gondola) as well as padding of seats, backs, and arms.

NEOCLASSICAL OR LOUIS XVI STYLE: HOTEL KAISERHOF, LADIES' PARLOR. The neoclassical style was already popular before the reign of Louis XVI (1774–1793), although it is associated with him. A chief feature of the neoclassical or Louis XVI style is a return to classical qualities, especially rectilinearity, order, and balance. Ceilings and walls can once again be distinguished. They are compartmentalized and may be decorated with plaster relief. Even though the colors in this room are not Louis XVI, which are soft pastels with one dominating color, it is designed as an ensemble, a feature that continues from earlier styles. Chair and table legs are straight, like Louis XIV style, but now they are light, graceful, and frequently shaped like fluted spindles. Occasional mirrors are also in keeping with the Louis XVI style. (CT.)

Three

Central Business District and North Loop

Initially Chicago's business district was located in a swath of land running east from Lake Michigan and west to the south branch of the Chicago River. Lake Street formed the major commercial strip, while industries requiring more land located farther north, south, and west. Only wealthy Chicagoans could afford living within the district, although African Americans and German and Irish immigrants lived at undesirable fringes near railroad depots. Even as commercial niches developed elsewhere, this land remained Chicago's thriving central business district.

Massive rebuilding immediately following the Great Fire of 1871 did little to change these patterns. Construction changed little as well. Because of the elevator, buildings grew as high as eight stories, but it took advances in steel and iron construction and improving foundation supports before structures soared to 16 to 18 stories, changing the business district dramatically. For another decade, businessmen dismissed the notion that valuable real estate should be allocated as public space. Even most of the wealthy found the central city too expensive, too commercial, and too crowded after the fire and chose to move.

The core of this district became known as the Loop when cable cars circled it in the late 1880s. After the elevated train connecting downtown and outlying neighborhoods looped around the district in 1897, the name was permanently embedded in Chicago's lexicon.

In 1908–1911, the city standardized street names and addresses. State Street divided the city east and west, and Madison Street divided it north and south. Hotels featured in this chapter extend from Madison Street north to the river and from the lake west to Desplaines Street.

NEW HOTEL GAULT (PRE-FIRE TO AROUND 1950.) The original Gault House was located at the northeast corner of West Madison and Clinton Streets. After surviving the 1871 fire, Gault House was sold the following day and immediately re-opened as "the 'Little' Sherman House." In 1911, the hotel was relocated at the southwest corner of Madison and Market Streets. This practically fireproof Italian Renaissance "New Gault House" had 10 rooms with shower baths, an innovation not yet a decade old. Chicago Mercantile Exchange occupies the site. (1915.)

THE STRATFORD HOTEL (1872–1922), LOBBY, SOUTHWEST CORNER, MICHIGAN AVENUE AND JACKSON STREET. Tufted leather Victorian circular sofas and potted plants are a focal point in this otherwise classically inspired lobby by W. W. Boyington. To the right of the entry are glass and wood cases filled with cigars, and four brass spittoons line the edges of the lobby.

The Stratford Hotel, Stratford Café. This postcard's sender reported he came to the elegant Stratford Café restaurant for toothpicks. In the 1900s, hotelkeepers debated whether to offer toothpicks. An industry leader advised fellow hoteliers that since "more than half" of their patrons used toothpicks, they ought to supply the humble article—providing they offered a toothpick of a good grade, which were not expensive. Those that splintered were "an abomination." (1908.)

The Stratford Hotel, New Dutch Room. Diners in this Old World restaurant heard music played by musicians on the mezzanine level just above. Some guests suggested those who liked music while dining could not carry on a conversation or were "so accustomed to the rattle of machinery or the clangor and ramble of street cars or other heavy traffic" they had grown uncomfortable with silence. Regardless, the music continued. (1908.)

HOTEL GRANT (1872–1940), NORTHWEST CORNER, DEARBORN AND MADISON STREETS. Originally a four-story structure housing the Chicago Savings Institution and Trust Company, two stories and a tower were added to Hotel Grant in 1901. The architects Adler and Sullivan repeated the 1872 simple Italianate style in the additional stories, but their own art comes through in the tower (compare with their Auditorium tower). Three First National Plaza is located on this site.

HOTEL GRANT, LOBBY. Guests could relax in the Windsor-style chairs, enjoying a cigar purchased from the humidor, or they could enter the buffet (right). Hoteliers of second-class properties bemoaned that travelers would often "spend Sundays and holidays and their money" at luxury hotels paying little attention to cost. But when these same patrons became budget-conscious and stayed at second-class hotels like this one, they would "grind and roast" the hoteliers for not offering more.

New Hotel Brevoort (1872–1906; Rebuilt 1906–Present), 120 West Madison Street. The New Hotel Brevoort was renovated in 1906 by architects H. R. Wilson and Benjamin H. Marshall. This 1906 reconstruction included an entire floor of sample rooms where, as in ancient inns, tradesmen conducted business. At the same time, and after years of debate, Northwestern Hotel Men's Association pledged to charge for the formerly free sample rooms. In 1953, the hotel was converted to offices and is now called 120 West Madison Street building. (1907.)

New Hotel Brevoort, Entrance. From the middle of the 19th century, more and more middle-class men became traveling salesmen (or "drummers"), merchants, accountants, bankers, physicians, managers, and secretaries for one of the new professional or trade associations. Like the men who linger here, many became guests at first- and second-class hotels, enjoying their bars and restaurants, barbershops and baths, billiard rooms, and writing rooms.

NEW HOTEL BREVOORT, PANEL PICTURE, LOBBY. Perhaps it was the attention to art—displayed throughout the hotel's public spaces like the lobby ceiling pictured here—that led Frank Lloyd Wright to live at this hotel before creating his Oak Park studio-home. Apollo holds his lyre as a muse and putti, or children with wings, accompany him.

NEW HOTEL BREVOORT, LOBBY. In 1901, several days after a guest checked in, his wife arrived. Late one night, seeing two people enter a room registered to one, a bellboy notified the front desk. Although the man informed the clerk the woman was his wife and it was only an oversight that he failed to register her, the coupled paid their bill and departed at 1 a.m., as the hotel demanded. Later the couple sued. Siding with the guests, the jury charged the hotel $1,000, $500 for each guest.

New Hotel Brevoort, Grill Room. Along the back wall of this feast-for-the-eye gentlemen's grillroom is a mural displaying elements of European life. Scottish clans were represented in a colored-glass window. Etched in the center of another window was a prayer of grace before meals by the poet Robert Burns: "Some hae meat and canna eat/And some wad eat tht want it/But we hae meat, and we can eat;/Sae let the Lord be thankit."

New Hotel Brevoort, Restaurant. In many ways, this is a generic classically-inspired restaurant with a bit of art nouveau topping it off in the curve of the back of the chairs. The room is an example of the way classicism can feel a little dull—too orderly and restrained. This postcard is one of the earliest printed, issued from 1898 to 1901 and called a private mailing card. (1907.)

New Hotel Brevoort, Buffet. For the 1893 fair, the hotel's circular crystal bar, reached only through the gentlemen's grill, dazzled patrons. In this equally lavish, Moorish-inspired 1898 renovation, the room itself became circular. Rich colors, intricate mosaic patterns, and arches nearly forming horseshoes are all inspired by the Moors, who were thought to be exotic. Mirrors and classically designed pillars enhance the magical effects of lights and an electric fountain. The railing is cut glass, and the bar's glassware was a special pattern for the hotel.

New Hotel Brevoort, Cozy Corner, Rainbow Room. The mural *Hindu Pilgrims Preparing the Evening Meal on the Banks of the Ganges* enhances this cozy corner. A new addition to hotel restaurants at the beginning of the 20th century, cozy corners evoked ingle nooks of old English inns, kindling notions of warmth and cheerfulness.

COMMERCIAL HOTEL (1872–PRE-1949), NORTHWEST CORNER, LAKE AND DEARBORN STREETS. Known as covers, stationery envelopes were frequently used to advertise hotels, as here. In addition to a sketch of this handsome Venetian Renaissance-style hotel, the cover lists rates as well as names of the proprietors and manager, important to guests during this period. The building was later known simply as the Commercial building.

TREMONT HOUSE (REBUILT POST FIRE 1873–1937), SOUTHEAST CORNER, LAKE AND DEARBORN STREETS. As flames engulfed the Tremont during the 1871 fire, proprietor John B. Drake bought a hotel at Michigan and Congress, betting the building would escape the fire. It did and the next day Drake opened the temporary New Tremont House until this French-inspired six-story, 250-room building was ready in 1873, built on its original site.

SHERMAN HOUSE (1873–1911), NORTHWEST CORNER, RANDOLPH AND CLARK STREETS. Designed by architect W. W. Boyington after the 1871 fire, this eight-story, Second Empire structure of light brown Kankakee stone boasted 300 rooms and, together with the Grand Pacific and the Palmer House, was identified as one of the city's grand hotels. By the end of the 19th century, however, the Sherman House fell into a slump, earning the label "the 'deadest hotel' in town." Purchasing the hotel initially as an investment in 1902, Joseph Beifeld (Fort Dearborn) soon became proprietor and quickly returned the hotel to splendor. He bought new furnishings, china, and silver; added telephones in every room; and, with a new manager, "keyed up" every department. As early as 1903, newspapers reported banquets, social events, and business gatherings at the Sherman, becoming "headquarters of note" once again. (AH, 1909.)

SHERMAN HOUSE (1911–1925). Success continued for Beifeld. In 1911, he replaced the old building with this 15-story, 757-room Beaux Arts design by Holabird and Roche. Still innovating in 1915, Beifeld dared to open one of the first coffee shops or lunchrooms in a Chicago hotel. While other hoteliers feared lunchrooms might cheapen their properties, Beifeld was making a profit offering a simple menu and remaining open at all hours. (1912.)

Hotel Sherman and College Inn, Chicago
City Hall Square
Every Room with Bath and Running Ice Water

141—Hotel Sherman, Chicago
© CURT TEICH & CO., INC.

SHERMAN HOUSE (1925–1973; DEMOLISHED 1950S AND 1973). The 1924 redesign, again by Holabird and Roche, resulted in this fashionable tripartite neoclassical 23-story building and annex. Newspapers lauded the 1,600-room Sherman as the largest hotel west of New York (the Stevens would exceed this in 1927). The main building was demolished in the 1950s and the annex in 1973. The James R. Thompson Center now occupies this block. (CT.)

SHERMAN HOUSE, FEBRUARY 1915 CONVENTION. Using a postcard as a marketing tool, a business association surrounds its conventioneers in the grand hall's splendor, while on the reverse side, it enumerates the benefits of membership, "We are sending you this card that you may have a better idea of our organization. Membership almost doubled this week . . . Yours for better service, Freeland & Carr." (EA, 1915.)

SHERMAN HOUSE, COLLEGE INN. When he took over the Sherman House in 1902, Beifeld established a highly successful restaurant, the College Inn. By 1905, he created an identical restaurant on the South Side (pictured here). Good food and music were featured at both locations, while the bandleader at the Loop location wandered from conventional hotel music to introduce jazz sound, establishing the College Inn as a jazz venue through the 1920s. (1905.)

BRIGGS HOUSE (REBUILT POST FIRE 1873–1928), NORTHEAST CORNER, RANDOLPH STREET AND FIFTH AVENUE (WELLS STREET). When diners protested a sharing fee after splitting a meal, the Briggs House added this menu announcement, "Prices are as low as can be made . . . When a portion . . . is divided between two or more, we reserve the right to make an extra charge . . ." The 188 West Randolph building now occupies this site.

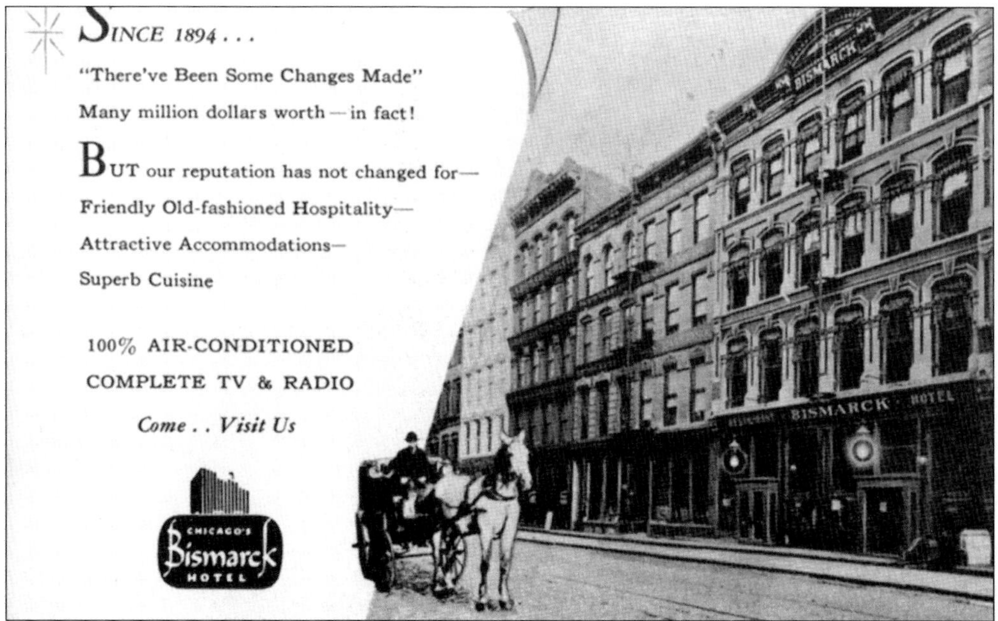

BISMARCK HOTEL (1894–1924), RANDOLPH, BETWEEN LASALLE AND WELLS STREETS. Following success as hoteliers in Hyde Park during the 1893 exposition, the enterprising brothers Emil and Karl Eitel assumed the management of a small, four-story Italianate hotel downtown, changing the name from Randolph to Bismarck Hotel to honor Germany's first chancellor. The Eitels expanded the property and strengthened the area as a civic and transportation center.

Bismarck Hotel (1926–Present). Plans for an entire city-block complex, including a 16-story hotel (right), 2,500-seat Palace Theater, and 22-story Metropolitan Office Building (left) emerged in 1926 from a design by architects Rapp and Rapp. In 1998, the Bismarck became part of the Kimpton Boutique Hotels under the name Hotel Allegro Chicago and continues operating today. (MRS.)

Bismarck Hotel, Main Restaurant and Bar. The décor—beer steins, murals, and *sgabelle* chairs (chairs created by adding a back to stools)—recalls the old country. This dining room led to a surprising nest of rooms reached only by passing from one to the next. At the end was the "farmhouse drinking room" featuring a mural—common in similar drinking rooms in Germany—painted by artists in gratitude for the proprietor's hospitality.

BISMARCK HOTEL, LADIES CAFÉ AND RESTAURANT. More formal than the previous restaurant, the Ladies Café and Restaurant also served as a banquet room. *Sgabelle* chairs are seen once again (see previous postcard). Murals of castles, ceilings embellished with ornamental patterns from ancient Rome and the Renaissance, and chandeliers with small electric lights create a festive, tasteful ambiance. (1905.)

BISMARCK HOTEL, WINTER GARDEN, AND BAUENSTUBE. A castle in the mountains and a half-timbered lodge bearing necessities of the hunt—rifles, horns, and shields—all conjure a journey to medieval times. Though not medieval, the chairs here are worthy of attention. Nicknamed "balloon" because of the shape of the back, they are inspired by the Prussian furniture designer Michael Thonet, creator of the bentwood rocker. One of the best designs of the times, this model was known officially as Classic Vienna Café. (1904.)

HOTEL LA SALLE (1908–1977), NORTHWEST CORNER, LASALLE AND MADISON STREETS. Named for the French explorer Sieur de LaSalle, this 22-story Beaux Arts hotel by Holabird and Roche with 1,048 rooms and a roof garden sought the well-to-do merchant, the tourist, and the capitalist who would appreciate and could afford the conveniences and luxuries of the modern hotel. Two years after its opening, a writer extolled the role this hotel played in reinvigorating the nightlife of its financial district location. "It has . . . increased the light zone of the down-town district, greatly benefited the neighboring property, and served to raise the realty values and create a new atmosphere and entirely new business for this part of town." In 1914, the hotel added the first multi-level garage with spiral ramp. A fire killed 61 people in 1946, prompting new building codes and firefighting procedures. The hotel recovered and continued until 1976. Two North La Salle is located here today. (1909.)

HOTEL LA SALLE, THE MAIN LOBBY. The grand lobby is inspired by French styles of Louis XIV, XV, and XVI that were popular during this era. Woven fabrics and rugs in rich gold tones, subdued browns, and bright greens highlight the space. A clock appears prominently in the grill above the clerk's desk, like that found in railroad depots. As was the intent of the palace of Versailles, a source for the French styles seen here, this interior confirms the guests' status as elites.

HOTEL LA SALLE, THE LOUIS XVI DINING ROOM. Featured in these pages are several of La Salle's dining rooms, ballrooms, and banquet rooms. Critics scoffed as the hotel was being constructed that it would never prosper with so many dining rooms, but—for over a half-century—the critics were wrong. (1917.)

HOTEL LA SALLE, THE BLUE FOUNTAIN ROOM. When hotels instituted the position of coat-checker in 1910, guests complained about tipping both coat checkers and waiters. Sometimes hoteliers sympathized with guests, and at other times they railed that if guests wanted "to have their coat secure," they needed to help pay for it. Few patrons today question tipping both. (1913.)

HOTEL LA SALLE, *THE THREE GRACES*, BLUE FOUNTAIN ROOM. A festive feeling is conveyed in this dining room through ribbed ceiling, intricate stapwork, a fountain, and several copies of classical statues, including *The Three Graces* by Antonio Canova's (1757–1822) and the Greek *Venus of Medici* (above). The trellis behind the Graces conjures perhaps a Renaissance garden. The room received its name from the blue light that would shine on the fountain.

La Salle, Red Room. While the purpose of grand rooms like this was to allow guests to do as they pleased, after a club was compelled to send its 500 guests a letter of apology "for off-color entertainment" during a program at a hotel banquet hall, hoteliers were urged to do more. Hotel leaders advised hoteliers to set an example of proper speech, demand employees to do likewise, provide more direction to entertainment committees, and join the Anti-Profanity League. (1919.)

Hotel La Salle, the Donatello Fountain, Palm Room. New York's Waldorf-Astoria established its fine dining room, the Palm Room, as the utmost in elegance and display. Soon other hotels found it a necessity to combine "columns, palms, lattice, greenery, running water, stained glass ceiling, and brilliant lighting" to create their own Palm Room, as did Hotel La Salle. Charming to some and irritating to others, the music from an orchestra playing near the lobby could be heard in this fine dining room.

HOTEL LA SALLE, THE BUFFET. The brass spittoons, or cuspidors, in this otherwise old English room were a 19th-century addition. Whether to include spittoons was debated among hoteliers. Advising all travelers should be accommodated, hotel leaders added that spittoons need not be conspicuous, but "they must be near at hand in public rooms."

HOTEL LA SALLE, THE GERMAN ROOM. While diners could order German dishes like pig's knuckle with sauerkraut, they could also feast on snails a la Bourguignonne, grilled lamb with sweet potatoes, grilled brook trout, and New England boiled fowl. The electric grill (left), where food ordered by diners was cooked, was a novelty at the time—and allowed the restaurant to be called a grillroom officially.

HOTEL LA SALLE, THE WRITING ROOM. A heroic-sized portrait of the hotel's namesake, Sieur de La Salle, dwarfs the fireplace in this English-inspired writing room. In addition to the refectory table for several writers, the hotel provided individual writing desks. When locals began to occupy desks like these to the exclusion of hotel guests, hoteliers moved to roll-top desks, providing keys to registered guests and rendering the desks inaccessible to freeloaders. The hotel provided stenographers, telephone booths, and other business services.

HOTEL LA SALLE, PARLOR PRESIDENTIAL SUITE. This French-inspired room is crowded with finely upholstered chairs, a settee, writing desk, central serving table, gilded mirror with a flourishing swag above the white fireplace, and a piano. Pianos were not unusual in guest parlors within first-class hotels, and guests would frequently move their activities from public parlors to these private ones. (1910.)

HOTEL PLANTERS, CLARK AND MADISON STREETS. Designed by John O. Pridmore in 1910, this nine-story classical structure blends the architectural ideas of both Chicago construction and Beaux Arts. Columbia Burlesque theater marquee announces its show, *The Flirting Widow*. Previously the Rose Sydell London Belles performed. The burlesque house became the Clark movie theater when the hotel was renamed the Harding. Three First National Plaza is located on this site. (CT, 1914.)

HOTEL PLANTERS, RESTAURANT/MERRIE GARDEN. In the early years, the Planter's restaurant was a classically inspired fine-dining room that included a small orchestra pit. By 1917, the restaurant was modified. Guests ate in the Merrie Garden and were entertained by cabaret acts like Gail Hambleton and Girls singing "Bachelor Days" and Delilah Leitzel and Boys singing "Flora Belle." In time, the room was redesigned in a medieval theme.

Four

Central Business District and South Loop

While Chicago's first business district was established a block south of the Chicago River along Lake Street, the rising commercial, manufacturing, financial, and retail businesses brought more and more people to the city. In an enterprising move following the Civil War, Potter Palmer located his new hotel on State Street at Madison Street and encouraged others, including Marshall Field, to relocate there as well. The commercial orientation shifted from east-west along Lake Street to north-south along State Street, where there was unobstructed expansion for growth.

For decades, hotels located closest to the heart of business activity were the most prestigious. But when the Auditorium opened in 1889, it suddenly made its locations away from the Loop more appealing, for it proudly announced guests would be beyond the horrid din of noise, the stench of smoke, and the filth of soot.

Not all were so fortunate, however. Most African Americans who moved to Chicago following Reconstruction in 1877 faced discrimination in housing, employment, and public accommodations. Prejudice in the city had already started to confine blacks to specific areas of the city. A fire in 1874 sent those living at the south end of the business district near Van Buren Street further south to Twenty-second and State Streets, an area that became part of the 33-by-3-block strip soon to be known as the Black Belt (and later as the Black Metropolis and, still later, Bronzeville).

Over several decades, this business district expanded south to Fourteenth Street and west to Desplaines Street, reaching the railroad depots. This change was well on its way at the time of the 1871 fire.

PALMER HOUSE (1873–1926), SOUTHEAST CORNER, STATE AND MONROE STREETS. Paying crews to work overnight, Palmer boasted his was the first post-fire construction and fireproof hotel. An astute businessman, Palmer persuaded the wealthy to leave their mansions and stay as residents, their regular payments helping when transient occupancy was low. The most renowned of Chicago's grand hotels, its lobby was the place to see and be seen—critical for those who aimed to wield power in the culture of conspicuous display and consumption. The Palmer House was designed by John Van Osdel with others.

PALMER HOUSE, DINING ROOM. Reportedly reproduced "almost exactly" as a dining room in Paris, this resplendent restaurant serving 1,000 stood apart. Soaring Corinthian columns set off stunning chandeliers whose glass bulbs recall papyrus flowers. In the late 1800s, when many hotels pointedly advertised their waiters were white, the Palmer House employed African Americans. (NYP.)

PALMER HOUSE, GENTLEMEN'S GRILL. In an era when many chefs and proprietors printed their menus in French, a leading journal in the hotel industry praised the Palmer House for using English. And in 1912, the hotel industry praised Potter Palmer, dead for a decade, for being the first to include American wines in his restaurants. (ECK.)

PALMER HOUSE (1926/1927–PRESENT). Open during the construction of its new building, the Palmer House claims today it is the oldest continuously operating hotel. In 1926, the 24-story building by Holabird and Roche contained over 2,250 rooms, occupying half a city block. In 1945, Conrad Hilton bought the hotel and in 1967 launched a three-year, $12 million modernization, adding convention halls, a swimming pool, and Palmer House Towers—luxury accommodations on the top two floors. In 1996, the lobby ceiling was restored to its original grandeur with 21 paintings of mythological scenes.

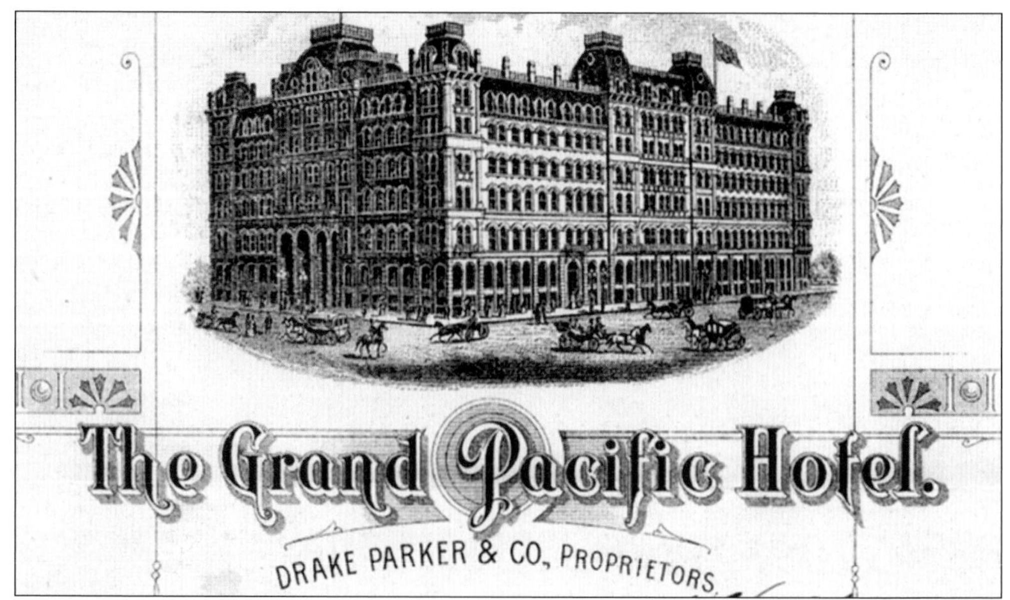

THE GRAND PACIFIC HOTEL (1873–1895), CLARK, QUINCY, LASALLE, AND JACKSON STREETS. John B. Drake managed this grand hotel by architect W. W. Boyington for more than 20 years, 1874–1895. His Great Game Dinners were one of Chicago's social institutions for more than 50 years. Newspapers devoted four inches to the 1890 menu, identified a long list of guests, and raptured over the "ornamental confectionery work." A sugar miniature of the Grand Pacific Hotel office, with likenesses of the desk clerks, awed guests and journalists most.

THE GRAND PACIFIC HOTEL (1895/8–1921). With the west section demolished for the Illinois Trust and Savings Building, the smaller, "more symmetrical and compact" Grand Pacific, designed by Jenney and Mundie, opened March 12, 1898, with 188 rooms. In his 1911 novel *Jennie Gerhardt*, Theodore Dreiser identified the Grand Pacific as "the exclusive hotel of the city." The hotel was finally razed in 1921 for the Continental Illinois Bank building. (1912.)

THE GRAND PACIFIC HOTEL, EMPIRE ROOM. In keeping with the Victorian penchant for something new and exciting, each of the hotel's 15 dining rooms was in a different style, including English, Dutch, French, Egyptian, Italian, Indian, Elizabethan, and Louis XVI. While called the Empire Room, the colors here are primarily Louis XVI—cream and soft blue accented with a Victorian-green carpet. (EA, 1913.)

WINDSOR-EUROPEAN HOTEL, DEARBORN, BETWEEN MADISON AND MONROE STREETS. In advertising accommodations for the 1893 exposition, proprietor Samuel Gregsten announced that he ". . . wishes the public to understand that no advances in rates will be charged other than has always been made . . . This house is patronized by respectable people only. No rooms for dudes, gamblers, drunken horse-dealers, or any persons inclined to be fast. The Windsor is a second-class hotel but has first-class patronage."

WINDSOR-CLIFTON HOTEL (1873–1927), NORTHWEST CORNER, MONROE STREET AND WABASH AVENUE. Designed by John M. Van Osdel and originally the Clifton House, the hotel's name changed when purchased in 1900 by Samuel Gregsten (Windsor European). Although close to shopping, some, like the sender of this postcard, were drawn to experience other charms, "Hello George! Suppose you have had a fine time out [at] the lake. Well! I have too—mixed up with the dirt and grime of Chicago . . . " Carson, Pirie Scott and Company's expansion occupies this corner of the block. (1907.)

VICTORIA HOTEL (1875–1908), NORTHWEST CORNER, MICHIGAN AVENUE AND VAN BUREN STREET. Originally this elegant Italianate structure was home to some of the city's most desirable bachelors. Built in 1875 as the Beaurivage Bachelor Apartments, it was renovated in 1892 and reopened as the 300-room Victoria. The McCormick Building now sits on this site. (VOH, 1912.)

HOTEL DE JONGHE, NORTH SIDE OF MONROE STREET, BETWEEN STATE STREET AND WABASH AVENUE. This small six-story Gothic-style structure built in 1876 was a downtown site for the new, hot, and controversial music—jazz—and great cuisine, including Shrimp De Johnge. Originally a private club with sleeping rooms, De Jonghe purchased the building in 1893, turning it into a hotel, music, and dining venue. The building was designed by architects Treat and Foltz.

SARATOGA HOTEL (BUILT 1879), A NOON HOUR IN THE SARATOGA HOTEL-RESTAURANT, 27 SOUTH DEARBORN STREET. Most meals were held in plain view, but some for a selected few were not. In the early 1900s, the Saratoga's attic was the scene for maverick "beefsteak feasts." Diners ate without knife, fork, or spoon on tables improvised from packing boxes and chairs. Those in the know said these events were followed by "the old-fashioned dances that our grand-parents tell about." (CT.)

The Morrison Hotel (1883–1912), Southeast Corner, Madison and Clark Streets. Initially four stories, the Morrison Hotel expanded to eight with increasing popularity among elites. Harry C. Moir, manager of the popular Boston Oyster House (under awning, left), secured a controlling interest around 1903. He renovated and expanded the hotel and purchased nearby property. Continued success inspired Moir to build from the ground up. (1908.)

The Morrison Hotel and Terrace Garden (1914–1925). Plans were drawn up in 1911, calling for a tower reaching 30-plus stories, but a city ordnance limited the height of buildings. In 1914, Moir opened the pictured 21-story structure designed by Marshall and Fox. While the 1914 construction included mechanical equipment and kitchens to service the expanded building, it appears no additional construction took place until 1925. (GB, 1925.)

THE MORRISON HOTEL (1925 TO AROUND 1966). In 1925, the Morrison expanded again, this time engaging Holabird and Roche. Although twin towers were planned, advertised, and shown on postcards, only one was built. The single 46-story tower on the right with an observation deck and flagpole soared to 637 feet. The hotel contained a total of 2,500 rooms. Chase Tower occupies the site today. (CT, 1947.)

THE MORRISON HOTEL, LOBBY, SHOWING MEZZANINE FLOOR. Signs in this classically inspired, luxurious lobby helped guests find their way to restaurants—Terrace Garden (left) and Grill Room (center). The "paging" system in the 1900s drew attention to guests in grand lobbies like this. A bellboy or page passed through the lobby and mezzanine calling the name of the guest who needed to be found. If there was no answer, the paging would be repeated at "frequent intervals" until the guest answered. (CC, 1922.)

THE MORRISON HOTEL, A GROUP OF "MURAL" ROOM WAITRESSES, BOSTON OYSTER HOUSE. Forty-three waitresses are pictured, each with their Gibson Girl upswept hairdo, high-collared white blouse, and dark skirt. An admirer of the service wrote in 1908 guests were attended by those "keyed to their work by both eye service and system; and rare indeed, it is, that a patron has any cause for complaint . . . the Boston Oyster House comes very near giving satisfaction all the time."

THE MORRISON HOTEL, A PRIVATE DINING ROOM. While this private dining room appears small, it was one of many on the hotel's second and third floors. Partitions could be opened and rooms quickly expanded. Each of the rooms was connected by a foyer to the grand banquet hall, with the total space accommodating more than 2,000 people.

The Morrison Hotel, Terrace Garden Ice Skating. This postcard offers a glimpse of the amusements the Morrison offered patrons, whether travelers or city residents. Guests could watch an ice show one evening and on another join their partners on a dance floor. (C.)

Hotel Victoria (Built 1885), Clark and Van Buren Streets. Known as the McCoy after its proprietor until 1910, this seven-story chateauesque hotel was a favorite Irish gathering place. Originally designed by Gregory Vigeant, an 1897 renovation added steam heat, hot and cold running water, electricity, parlors, and a renovated lobby. Not to be caught off guard, this "dean of hoteliers" installed boilers, dynamos, and pumps in duplicate. When McCoy retired, the name changed to Hotel Victoria (different from the Victoria Hotel). The Chicago Stock Exchange Extension building occupies this site.

HOTEL GRACE (1887/1889–PRE-1990), SOUTHEAST CORNER, JACKSON AND CLARK STREETS. When no hotelier jumped at the leasing price of $17,000, Edward Grace decided to manage the hotel he had built, designed by John M. Van Osdel. In spite of Grace's having no experience, the hotel became well known for exquisite meals and a most handsome banquet hall. The Metcalf Federal Center building occupies this site. (HGZ, 1908.)

HOTEL KAISERHOF (1889–1915), 320–328 SOUTH CLARK STREET. Although the architect is unknown, the 1889 building reflects the concerns of well-known Chicago architects, starting with the rusticated stone. The sense of movement and rhythm from bottom to top indicates an awareness of the importance of creating a unified whole. Still, the awkward stacking of the top three floors indicates this architect had not yet solved the problem of the tall building. During World War I, the hotel's name changed to the Atlantic.

Hotel Kaiserhof (1915–1971), 314–318 Clark Street. This 18-story tower of steel and concrete by Marshall and Fox added 238 rooms, doubling the total. With the post office, Board of Trade, and three railroad depots nearby, an observer of Chicago's hotels noted at the tower's opening, "The location of the Kaiserhof hotel is growing better all the time." (MRS.)

Hotel Kaiserhof, Lobby. America's first hoteliers outfitted hotel lobbies to mirror parlors in mansions so local wealthy residents would feel comfortable and support the new enterprise. By the 1900s, however, hoteliers were irritated with too many residents lounging in their lobbies and wrote to "chair boarders" to spend their leisure time elsewhere. But hoteliers had a difficult time enforcing their request: they were still complaining in 1910 that guests too often could not find available seats. (CT.)

HOTEL KAISERHOF, LADIES' DINING ROOM. The imposing, soft-rose columns in this alluring room are striking on their own, but spectacular, Sullivanesque embellishments explode at their capitals. Golden chandeliers with small, beguiling lights are among the most engaging in all hotel interiors and again have a Sullivan-like touch. (CT, 1906.)

HOTEL KAISERHOF, *Bauern Stube*. It is possible to roll back time and eavesdrop on a 1913 meeting of Chicago hotel stewards at the Kaiserhof where the Blackstone's Jacob Straub has reported that the whiskey most stewards bought was likely "rectified." Federal law allowed bogus whisky to be made if distillers paid a tax "rectifying" what they had done. Stewards could check the validity of what they were purchasing by looking for a green government stamp on the cork of each bottle. (CT.)

THE AUDITORIUM (1890–PRESENT), NORTHWEST CORNER, MICHIGAN AVENUE AND CONGRESS STREET. Reeling from the aftermath of the 1886 Haymarket Riot, businessman Ferdinand Peck aimed to transform the animosity and hysteria between owners and workers by building a music hall, reflecting Peck's profound faith in the power of art. To ensure its economic survival, Peck planned to construct not just a music hall but an entire complex of theater, hotel, stores, and restaurants. Just days after the riot, Peck persuaded leaders to back the enterprise in an unprecedented coalescing of sources, one that led Congress to award Chicago the prestigious right to host the 1893 World's Columbian Exposition. Despite its acclaim with the public, by the 1920s the complex was "deviled by debt and taxes" and by 1929 went bankrupt. Following its service in the Second World War as a USO headquarters, Roosevelt University purchased the Auditorium, renovating the hotel for administrative offices and classrooms while restoring several public rooms including the Sullivan Room (ladies parlor) and Ganz Hall (small banquet hall). (1911.)

THE AUDITORIUM, THEATER. To create a superb theater, Peck chose architect Dankmar Adler, a virtuoso in acoustics. Accompanying Adler was young Louis Sullivan. Adler produced a theater whose acoustics remain the best in the city, but it was Sullivan, soon renowned for his dictum "form follows function," who gave Peck's political commitments and faith in art physical form. Sullivan designed a hall so large that for it to be financially successful, no one group could fill it. Those in the least and most costly seats were equally close to the performers, and the stage was so flexible the Auditorium could present both solo performers and grand operas. While not achieved, Peck's grand vision set a broader social and cultural agenda than any previously crafted. His commitment to cultural democracy continues: renovated by the university, the theater is in daily use today as a rock 'n roll arena, a Broadway theater, a dance performance hall, and a community venue. Although perhaps not quite as Peck envisioned, wealthy, working, and middle classes cross paths inside the Auditorium. Once in place, function follows form. (SU, 1906.)

THE AUDITORIUM, TOWER. The Auditorium and tower stood as a powerful symbol to the city from the start. Historian Mark Allan Clague comments that, as the tallest building of its day, the Auditorium represented Chicago's "I will" spirit and announced the city's importance to the Midwest, the nation, and the world. To outmaneuver the uneven settlement that plagued Chicago builders, Adler added weight to the foundation totaling the anticipated weight of the tower. As each floor was added, an equal weight was removed from the foundation. For 25¢, visitors were offered a "360-degree mesmerizing view of the city." Heavy black smoke often obliterated the view to the west and north, where most residents lived. But to the east, viewers could enjoy schooners, steamers, and yachts on Lake Michigan or scan the shoreline to Michigan, Indiana, and Wisconsin. To the south, viewers could thrill at the mansions of the wealthy. Sullivan's office, music studios, and arts organizations, among others, were tenants in the tower that today houses Roosevelt University faculty and administration. (MRS, 1916.)

THE AUDITORIUM, LOBBY. Lobbies in first-class hotels at the end of the 19th century were places to conduct business, socialize, and see and be seen, "What was on display was not simply an array of objects but also a lifestyle and social status." To confer such status, the lobbies themselves dazzled. For his lobby, Sullivan, however, refused to mimic European taste. To build the national character, he chose instead American raw materials and looked to nature as the model for his intricate designs carved in stone, metal, and wood. The space today is a lobby for Roosevelt University. (ECK.)

THE AUDITORIUM, SUMMER RESTAURANT. The actress Sarah Bernhardt stood on the hotel's second-floor balcony, gazed out over Michigan Avenue, amidst smokestacks, strolling pedestrians, street traffic, and the expanse of railroad lines, and proclaimed, "This is the pulse of America!"

AUDITORIUM, LADIES' ENTRANCE. From the time hotels emerged in the late 18th century, they represented one of the few respectable public places for women. Nonetheless, women also had limited access within hotels. Given their own entrance in most first-class hotels (here, first door on the left), women would not linger long in lobbies, which were men's spaces, but progressed quickly to their own parlors and restaurants. (Courtesy of Roosevelt University.)

THE AUDITORIUM, RESTAURANT. Originally the ladies restaurant, women entered from the ladies' reception room, mezzanine, or Congress Street. This room was lighter in atmosphere than any other in the hotel. Missing from this image are the room's exquisite electroliers or lights that "rose from the floor" on a single stem and burst open "like groups of daylilies." Partially destroyed by Congress Street widening in 1952, this room now houses Roosevelt University's admissions office. (MRS, 1917.)

The Auditorium, Banquet Hall. In this small, stunning hall hang 12 jewel-like electrolier lights, imbuing a radiant glow. The lights, birchwood columns, carved capitals, and stained art glass all compelled one writer to praise Sullivan as "a man whose creative powers seem inexhaustible, and who pours out original designs as water gushes from the rocks of the mountains." Roosevelt University restored this room to its original radiance and uses it as a recital hall. (Courtesy of Roosevelt University.)

The Auditorium, Banquet and Convention Room. Construction was already underway when the decision was made to add a dining room and kitchen. So they were added to the top of the building. This vented odors directly through the roof, away from other floors. The absence of obtrusive columns allowed for greater flexibility in setting the room for special events. Today this is Roosevelt University's library. (CT.)

Great Northern Hotel (1891–1940), Dearborn, Jackson, and Quincy Streets. Proprietor William S. Eden was first a barber at the Palmer House where he persuaded Palmer to inlay silver dollars in the barbershop floor. He did the same with a floor in his own hotel and the Silver Dollar Bar quickly became "one of the most exclusive spots," in this hotel designed by Burnham and Root. Dirksen Federal Center is now on this site. (CT, 1906.)

Great Northern Hotel, Café-Parlor Floor. While this room exemplifies Victorians' penchant for mixing styles with its classical drapery, baroque mirrors, and Eastern chandeliers, the chairs are of particular interest. They were likely inspired by Prussian Michael Thonet, who created the famous bentwood rocker. The upholstery on the seats and backs underscores the Victorian desire for additional comfort. A sender of this card sketched the happy diners on the right. (1911.)

GREAT NORTHERN HOTEL, NEW MAIL DEPARTMENT. "It will take some money, but it will be returned. Good mail service will do as much to enhance the reputation of a hotel as good beds or good table," so hoteliers were instructed. What a fine way to inform guests the hotel took their mail seriously—sending them a photograph of the innovative, fireproof (no less) mail department on a postcard. (1908.)

THE AUDITORIUM ANNEX/CONGRESS HOTEL (1893–PRESENT), 504–520 SOUTH MICHIGAN AVENUE. The 11-story Auditorium Annex was built three years after the Auditorium, yet its private baths made it more popular. Architects Holabird and Roche respected Clinton J. Warren's original design in nearly seamless 1902 and 1907 additions. The hotel became known as the Congress Hotel and Annex after a change in management. It operates today as the Congress Plaza Hotel and Convention Center. (VOH, 1908.)

CONGRESS HOTEL, LOBBY. This fanciful lobby is a good introduction to the hotel, for it exudes the passion for diverse styles executed in full splendor throughout. The lobby includes classical, Egyptian, and Moorish motifs. The low-to-the-ground, stuffed furniture, sprawling ferns, and overall visual excitement are pure Victorian sensibility. (ECK.)

CONGRESS HOTEL, BANQUET HALL. "The walls and ceiling are literally plastered with gold leaf. We do not know of any other large room anywhere that makes such a show of gold. About the only relief from it is a series of paintings in the ceiling," so a reporter noted—rather ecstatically—in 1907, when the room opened. The hall is still in use today for banquets, weddings, and convocations. The chandeliers are deceptively small in the postcard. Nearly twice the size as they appear, they are most imposing. (VOH.)

Congress Hotel, Peacock Alley/Marble Corridor. The term peacock alley originated in New York's Waldorf-Astoria hotel during the 1890s. To enter the Waldorf's fine dining Palm Room, guests strolled through a glassed-enclosed corridor, watched by spectators who perched themselves behind the glass. Soon identified as Peacock Alley "for all the strutting of fancy feathers that went on there," the idea spread to the nation's hotels. Congress's first Peacock Alley was located in a tunnel connecting the Auditorium and the Annex, where artists appearing at the theater could be seen. When the hotel added a new building in 1907, this Peacock Alley, connecting the north and south towers of the hotel, emerged. The corridor is still called Peacock Alley, although the chairs are gone. (VOH, 1912.)

CONGRESS HOTEL, JAPANESE TEA ROOM. Like others in the hotel, this exquisite room reflects an interest in the exotic. Created by Kawahe Studio, its design is based on temples of the 13th to 15th centuries and combines colors from both temples and private homes. More than 30 varieties of mums decorate the murals, and storks and trees are carved into wood panels. Its latticed ceiling is inset with gold metal ornaments and dark red tiles cover the floor accented by black marble near the walls. This room no longer exists. (VOH.)

CONGRESS HALL, FLORENTINE BANQUET HALL. The ceiling of this wood-paneled, softly illuminated room displays a series of grotesques. The term refers to decorations found in Roman grottos, not bizarre creatures in the word's modern definitions. While the room exists today, recent efforts to renovate the ceiling have been halted.

Congress Hotel, Pompeian Room. This room reflects both the great interest in the past that archeological digs at Pompeii and Herculaneum stirred among late-19th-century Americans and their lack of concern for accuracy. For example, while paintings were found on Pompeian walls, they did not look like those found here, and the sleek, square chairs and tall vases are Chinese rather than Pompeian. Nonetheless, the individual components blend together to create a stately, restful ambiance, and that is what the hotel guest sought. (DP, 1906.)

Congress Hotel, Fountain in Pompeian Room. The calming, grand Louis Comfort Tiffany fountain was at the edge of the original Pompeian room, but as the room was expanded, it came to rest in the center. The Pompeian Room and fountain have been lost. (DP.)

HOTEL MAJESTIC (1893–1961), 29 WEST QUINCY STREET AT STATE STREET. This 17-story building with undulating bay windows repeats the window patterns and general exterior of the Great Northern located behind the hotel. At the top of the building, by D. H. Burnham and Company, is a receding 16th floor capped by the final floor that includes the sky room. The Federal Center is now located here. (VOH.)

HOTEL MAJESTIC, THE SKY ROOM. Sweeping arches, panoramic views, and a high ceiling of art glass dominate this versatile room. Hoteliers' discussions about serving guests in grand banquet rooms like this expressed concern about the new practice of placing cocktails automatically at each person's place. Believing liquor ruined the taste buds, these naysayers advised cocktails be served only to those who asked for them, contending the cocktail was a mere fad.

YWCA HOTEL (1894–PRESENT), 830 SOUTH MICHIGAN AVENUE. Thirteen women gathered on December 12, 1876, to establish Chicago's first YWCA to help single white Christian women entering the city seeking work. By the 1890s, they needed larger facilities. For Herma Clark, who later wrote the 30-year *Chicago Tribune* column "When Chicago Was Young," the YWCA was her first home in the city. After serving multiple uses, including headquarters for Johnson Publications (*Ebony* and *Jet* magazines), the building, part of a landmark district, is currently vacant. John M. Van Osdel II, son of Chicago's first architect, was the designer. (VOH, 1910.)

HOTEL NORMANDIE, MICHIGAN AVENUE AND TWELFTH STREET. In a magazine for actors and theater-goers, this hotel boasted its Chicago-style construction by noting it is "A Thoroughly Modern Hotel Structure With Steam Heat, Electric Lights, Baths and Is Absolutely Fireproof." And it was a mere 10-minute walk to theaters.

THE BLACKSTONE (1908–PRESENT, CLOSED), SOUTH MICHIGAN AVENUE AND HUBBARD PLACE (BALBO AVENUE). A New York journalist lauded Blackstone as "outfitted finer than any hotel I have ever seen." Tracy and John Drake, sons of John B. Drake Sr., named the hotel and created a logo (a rooster and two railroad tracks) to honor Timothy B. Blackstone, a business associate of their father's who headed both the Chicago and Alton Railroad and Union Stockyards. Awarded the Gold Medal of the American Institute of Architects, Marshall and Fox's design also became a model for other hotels. Plans were developed for an annex, but these were dropped as World War I began. Mortgaging the Blackstone to maintain their new Drake Hotel, the Drakes lost ownership after the 1933 Century of Progress Exposition. Nonetheless, for decades, the Blackstone was identified as the "premier luxury hotel, and home for U.S. presidents, celebrities, and visiting royalty." The Beatles' guru Maharishi Mahesh Yogi was the last owner before closing. The building stands idle today, with asbestos and other problems stalling development.

THE BLACKSTONE, LOBBY SHOWING ENTRANCE. Successfully blending several interior styles, the luxurious lobby created an atmosphere of a great manor house of the 18th century with its dark wood walls and segmented ceiling. Separate elevators were available for guests arriving for functions in the ballroom and banquet rooms "so that social functions may be as exclusive as desired." (ML.)

THE BLACKSTONE, LOBBY SHOWING STEPS TO MAIN RESTAURANT. Other hotels may have offered far longer peacock alleys, but the Blackstone's wide, white statuary marble staircase demonstrates that display did not need a long expanse (see Congress, peacock alley). In an era valuing surprise and theatricality, guests no doubt thrilled at the dramatic difference between the dark, manorial lobby and the light, classically styled dining room just beyond these steps. (ML.)

The Blackstone, Main Restaurant. This room explodes with the opulence of the age and the desires of its proprietors in almost every element. The design starts with conventional, formal features and then plays with them, grandly. Bright, bold red abounds in the draperies, the rugs and, especially eye-dazzling, the backs and seats of the chairs. The generally subdued Roman arches have been wildly embellished, perhaps a Moorish or Asian inspiration. And there is not just a touch of ornamentation here and there. It bounces off arch after arch throughout the room. The white is so intense and stark, it is difficult to imagine a more explosive counterpoint to the red. As if all of this were not enough to reach a pinnacle of grandeur and display, the center window in the room framed the largest pane of glass in America: ah, to see and be seen. This room was also called American Beauty Room, perhaps not solely in reference to the rose but all those beauties—men and women—who sat down nightly at its tables. (ML.)

The Blackstone Hotel, Barbershop. Like the barbershops in the Palmer House and Auditorium, this barbershop is as glamorous as the hotel's other public rooms, bedecked with classical columns, latticed ceiling, red leather chairs with onyx frames, and white porcelain bowls. It also provided small rooms to guests wanting to change for dinner. The hotel noted its barbers were white in its brochures. (ML, 1913.)

The Blackstone, Banquet Room. After touring the Grand Pacific, John Willy, *Hotel Monthly* publisher, reported why he thought John Drake and his sons Tracy and John Jr. were superior hoteliers. From their father, the sons learned how to carve 23 orders from a turkey in just five minutes. When they got through, Willy noted, "there wasn't much of anything except bones left," adding the best hoteliers knew how to perform every job. The 100 guests soon to be served here were in good hands. (ML.)

The Blackstone, Large French Room. Guests might think hotel staff would grow arrogant about stellar performance, but steward Fred Muller's joy following a day of "record-breaking service" in 1916 is clear, "I am especially pleased at the smoothness of the dining room service. That, to me, has been a marvel . . . where we have so many dining rooms, and . . . banquet halls . . . all done with clockwork regularity, without friction; it is indeed something to feel good over." (ML.)

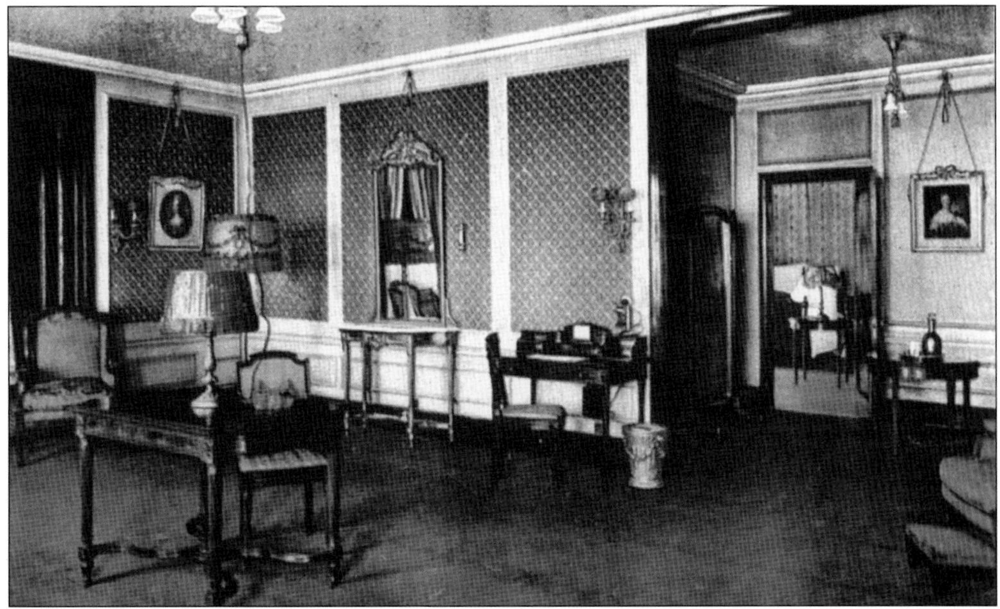

The Blackstone Hotel, Parlor and Bed Chamber. When guests entered, they would have appreciated immediately certain innovations, especially the telephone at the desk, essential in a first-class room. However, they often placed a call to the front desk unable to find the toilet hiding in the bathroom beneath an elegant mahogany chair, complete with cane back and cane seat—or toilet lid. (ML.)

YMCA HOTEL (1916–PRESENT), 826 SOUTH WABASH AVENUE. "The Y.M.C.A. hotel is not to be a competitor of the legitimate hotels of Chicago. It is intended to be a transient home for young men of all nationalities coming to the city, so they may have safe quarters at reasonable cost amid respectable surroundings, . . ." affirmed an article featuring the opening of Chicago's YMCA hotel, designed by Robert C. Berlin. Guests—limited to white men—could lodge for up to one month. The building has been converted to luxury condominiums called Burnham Plaza. (1916.)

YMCA HOTEL, CORNER OF MESSER MEMORIAL ROOM. This classically inspired room in the 1926 expansion features a club-like atmosphere with comfortable leather-upholstered armchairs and large refectory-style table like that offered in many hotel reading and writing rooms. (ECK.)

FORT DEARBORN HOTEL (1914–PRESENT), SOUTHEAST CORNER, LASALLE AND VAN BUREN STREETS. Two years after opening, president Joseph Beifeld (Sherman House) experimented with a "first-come, best-served" policy that most hoteliers railed against. Guests arriving early paid $1.50 for large rooms with baths, while late-arriving guests paid the same for rooms without baths. Fort Dearborn's practice did not win out. Since then, rates depend upon availability, size, location, and amenities. Closed in 1983 and converted to offices in 1985, the original Holabird and Roche structure was renamed the Traders Building. (CT.)

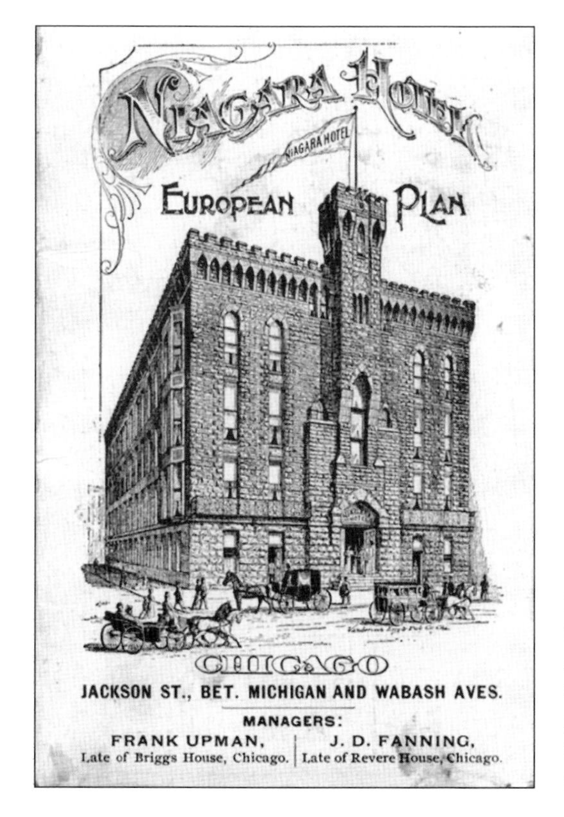

NIAGARA HOTEL, JACKSON STREET, BETWEEN MICHIGAN AND WABASH AVENUES. This quaint hotel, resembling a medieval castle, boasts in a charming pamphlet for guests to the 1893 exposition that it can be found in no less than "the bon ton [high style] location."

HOTEL MAYER (1892–PRESENT), WABASH AVENUE AT TWELFTH STREET (ROOSEVELT ROAD). Built for the 1893 exposition, guests in later decades took full advantage of the city's cultural events. As this visitor writes, "Needless to say we will be glad to be home again. 3 matinees & night show, so you see how much time we have." Today this Chicago construction-style building is being transformed into apartments.

HOTEL LOMBARD (1914–1959), NORTHEAST CORNER, FIFTH (WELLS AVENUE) AND QUINCY STREETS. Clean, sleek lines stress the horizontal rather than the vertical of this 11-story building by D. H. Burnham and Company. Located opposite Continental Commercial Bank, one of the largest office buildings in Chicago at the time, the hotel included 200 rooms with private baths and 50 sample rooms for salesmen and their customers. An addition to the Federal Reserve Bank is now located here.

Five

Near North and North Side

Beginning at the Chicago River, the poorest part of the city, Near North contained the city's first industries and railroad. The 1871 fire destroyed the homes but left most industries intact allowing for a quick recovery. When Potter and Bertha Palmer built their castle-like home along Lake Shore Drive in 1882, they began a trend during which wealthy Chicagoans joined them in establishing exclusive homes and creating the famous Gold Coast, the inner city's most prestigious neighborhood. As the eastern part of Near North developed, the western district grew poorer, becoming known in the 1880s as Smokey Hollow due to industry pollution, and Death's Corner, because of crime.

Lakefront property above North Avenue served as a cemetery from the city's incorporation until the mid-1860s when it became Lincoln Park. Following the fire, the wealthy built mansions fronting the park while middle-class commuters found homes along the elevated rail lines, and industries, including furniture and farm equipment manufacturing, hugged the river, attracting ethnic workers.

From Fullerton Avenue north to Devon, Chicago's first north-shore suburb was incorporated as Lakeview township in 1875 and annexed by the city in 1889. Its early residents were predominantly celery farmers from Germany, Sweden, and Luxemburg. In 1886, John Lewis Cochran bought land in the northern part of the township, creating Edgewater and building mansions for the wealthy along the lakefront and smaller homes to the west. After the Northwestern Elevated Railroad was extended to Wilson Avenue in 1900, Cochran worked to continue the line, first to Bryn Mawr Avenue and then, in 1908, to Howard Street, resulting in the development of hotels and apartments along the corridor.

Lake View House (1853/1854–1890), Northwest Corner, Byron (Grace) Street and Lakefront. Built by James Rees and Elisha Hundley to accommodate potential home buyers and those overseeing their new construction, this lakefront hotel was admired as "quite a watering place . . . destined to become the Saratoga of Illinois." The hotel and community's name was suggested by library founder Walter L. Newberry as he stood on the veranda. (Courtesy of the Chicago History Museum.)

Revere House (1874–1949), Southeast Corner, Clark and Hubbard Streets. This largely Italianate 170-room hotel featured a newfangled gadget called an elevator. Its guests included the jury of the Haymarket Riot Trial during the summer of 1886 as well as actors Wallace Berry and Gloria Swanson, who lived here when Chicago was the center of the silent film industry. A fire on December 9, 1948, forced its closure. (CTP, 1912.)

THE ALEXANDRIA (BUILT 1891), SOUTHWEST CORNER, RUSH AND OHIO STREETS; THE BRADLEY (BUILT 1892), NORTHWEST CORNER, RUSH STREET AND GRAND AVENUE. Both hotels follow many of the design principles known as Chicago construction. Designed by Edmund R. Krause, the Alexandria, formerly the Granada, added seven stories along Ohio Street in 1914. The Bradley, known for its "stylish but affordable" apartments, opened as the DuBuque, later called Milner, and finally the Chicagoan. (CT, 1934.)

ONTARIO HOTEL (1881–1965) SOUTHWEST CORNER, STATE, AND ONTARIO STREETS. One of Chicago's earliest apartment buildings, heated by fireplaces in every room and featuring the service of a single telephone (in the basement), the Ontario, designed by Treat and Foltz, was converted into a hotel for the 1893 exposition and remained an apartment hotel thereafter. It featured the American room-and-board plan long after other hotels adopted the European Plan separating room and board. (1910.)

NEWBERRY HOTEL, 817 NORTH DEARBORN STREET. In 1905, proprietor Pearl Billings commented that "while we never advertise, the hotel is full nearly all of the time with transients . . . We have 125 rooms and the house count is 140. This is pretty good for a hotel located in a residential district." It was located next to the extant houses for the Newberry Estate and the former Grant's Seminary for Young Ladies. (ECK, 1910.)

HOTEL LEGRAND, NORTHWEST CORNER, KINZIE AND WELLS STREETS. Established in 1875 and rebuilt in 1889, this 1896 postal cover notes that the 125-room hotel was located opposite the North Western Depot (where the Merchandise Mart stands today) and featured electric call bells, a passenger elevator, telephone service, and "all modern improvements."

LUZERNE HOTEL, NORTH CLARK AND CENTRE (ARMITAGE) STREETS. Above the entrance—which is located in the center segment of this seven-sectioned building—is the hotel's sign. From there, the eye is directed upward to the neo-gothic pediment and unfurled flag at the roofline. Like many first- and second-class hotels, the first floor was devoted to retail space, including a pharmacy (corner) and the Nichols brothers' real estate company (right of entrance). (1911.)

VIRGINIA HOTEL. (1889/1890–1929), NORTHWEST CORNER RUSH AND OHIO STREETS. McCormick Harvesting Machine Company's cofounder, Leander J. McCormick, built this 480-room hotel designed by Clinton J. Warren. "Removed from the noise, dirt and confusion of the business district it was within easy walking distance" of the railroads and Lake steamers that shuttled to and from the 1893 fair. In 1906, the hotel boasted that it possessed an air cleaning plant that removed dust from floors, walls, draperies, and furniture "w/out polluting the air in the rooms." (CT.)

Plaza Hotel (1892–1965), 1553 North Clark Street. With 600 rooms spread among 150 apartments, this was one of Chicago's early apartment hotels. Designed by Clinton J. Warren, and resembling his Michigan Avenue hotels, Metropole and Lexington, the Plaza was divided into three equal sections separated by narrow light courts providing light into two or three sides of every apartment. The exclusive Latin School of Chicago now occupies the site. (GB.)

Plaza Hotel, Lobby and Office. Residential services included "electric light, heat, bell boy and janitor service, repairs, window cleaning, scrubbing and some other minor privileges" according to a 1901 magazine. Chambermaid service was contracted at 15¢ per hour through the head housekeeper, who retained a portion for her fee. Chambermaids worked an 8:00 a.m.-to-4:00 p.m. shift and earned $4–$6 per week. (CTP, 1914.)

THE BREWSTER HOTEL (1893–PRESENT), NORTHWEST CORNER, DIVERSEY, AND PINE GROVE AVENUES. This striking, eight-story building designed by Enoch Hill Turnock combines H. H. Richardson's Romanesque style and rustication with Chicago construction in a tripartite manner. Each unit opens onto a court of glass block, allowing light to stream down through the rooftop atrium. The building is faced with quartzite and topped with a highly decorative cornice. The ladies entrance, now the main entrance, was located on Pine Grove Avenue.

SHENENDOAH HOTEL, SUNNYSIDE AND KENMORE AVENUES. This handsome building, located north of Graceland Cemetery, mixes Chicago construction style with a Queen Anne tile roof. The terms apartment and hotel began to blur by the late 19th century, and apartment hotel indicated a residence with hotel services and furnishings for both transient and permanent guests. (1912.)

Edgewater Beach Hotel (1916–1967), 5300 North Sheridan Road. Designed by Marshall and Fox, and built in the form of a Greek cross, the Edgewater Beach became one of Chicago's most famous resorts and convention hotels. When it opened, *Hotel Monthly* described it as "a suggestion of Atlantic City. Located directly at the water's edge . . . green lawn on all sides; beach walk; boulevard alive with pleasure automobiles; rates charged according to season . . . sun parlors galore (2 at the end of each wing) . . . tea rooms, ball rooms, balcony promenades; the home of wealth, luxury, freedom of household cares." (VOH.)

Edgewater Beach Hotel Addition (1923–1967). Built between 1923 and 1926, the 19-story high-rise tower was stepped symmetrically in the middle to complement the original building, creating 1,000 guest rooms. This card is part of a larger fold-up postcard containing a menu for the American Bankers Association banquet in the South Room. Among the menu items were Cantaloupe Edgewater Beach and Bankers Salad. (CT, 1926.)

EDGEWATER BEACH HOTEL, PASSAGIO. This *passagio*, or passageway, functions like the musical term—a series of notes in which a transition occurs. Here the transition is between the hotel's public spaces. The passagio connected the old hotel with the new tower while providing access to the main ballroom, Edgewater Room, and East Lounge. In the front left corner sits a writing desk with paper and pen at the ready. (CT.)

EDGEWATER BEACH HOTEL, ENTRANCE. Balustrades overflowing with tropical plants and terraces of potted flowers grace the impressive entrance. This main entrance was in the original building leading guests to the center of the cruciform and the main lobby. Throughout its operation, the hotel provided transportation to Marshall Field's department store downtown. Later the hotel offered seaplane service to the Loop, and in the 1960s, helicopter service to Chicago's O'Hare airport. (AC.)

Edgewater Beach Hotel, Dining Room. This unusual double card shows the expansiveness of the dining room in a panoramic view. The view prompted the hotel to advertise "every seat [a] commanding water view." Formal banquettes line both walls, and an open area of dancing is

Edgewater Beach Hotel, East Lounge. Across the passagio from the ballroom, guests arrived at the East Lounge through a Palladian entrance. The room's clerestoried cathedral ceiling provides an English Renaissance atmosphere to the room. A model of a 16th-century ship sits on the table in the foreground. (CT.)

at the center. Eventually referred to as the "Marine Dining Room," this was the hotel's formal, fine dining room, accommodating up to 1,200 people when connected with the adjoining South Lounge. (ECK.)

EDGEWATER BEACH HOTEL, FLOWER SHOP. Floral arrangements, corsages, and potted plants of all types were conveniently available in this store. Additional shops and personal services, including a beauty salon, barbershop, and sauna, were located throughout the ground floor. A former hotel employee recalls that the hotel had its own upholstery shop and would change rugs and upholstery in the lounges and lobbies seasonally—a set for winter and a set for summer. (AC.)

Edgewater Beach Hotel, Beach Walk. The Beach Walk, peaking in the 1940s and 1950s, provided one of the most famous venues for outdoor dancing, refreshments, entertainment, and open-air concerts. The expansion of Lake Shore Drive in the 1950s cut the hotel off from the lake and its 1,200-foot private beach, ending its attraction as a resort. The Breakers, a modern residential tower, is now here. (AC.)

Edgewater Beach Hotel and Apartments (1929–Present). With the hotel painted light yellow and the apartments (far right) pink, the resort became a noticeable and well-loved landmark. This card shows the breadth of the complex that is connected by swimming pools, tennis courts, and a golf course. The apartment building, a 20-story residential high-rise with a variety of retail shops and services on the first floor, is the sole surviving element of the complex. (CT.)

Six

Near South and South Side

During the 1840s and 1850s, working-class German, Irish, and Scandinavians lived between Twelfth and Thirty-ninth Streets, working at nearby railroads, lumber mills, and stockyards. But by the 1860s and 1870s, wealthy Chicagoans began building mansions along Prairie Avenue and the boulevards south of Sixteenth Street.

Yet in 1882, Potter and Bertha Palmer left their Prairie Avenue home and built a mansion north of downtown, in what many thought at the time was a foolish move. But their premonition of the neighborhood's changing face came true when, in anticipation of the 1893 World's Columbian Exposition, a building frenzy led to hotels, apartments, and elevated railroads. By the late 1890s, the wealthy had abandoned the district, and their homes and hotels passed first into the hands of working-class Europeans and then, by the second decade of the 20th century, to African Americans. While African Americans began to operate hotels in the area, it is not until the after the Depression that a historical record regarding these venues emerges.

Four miles southwest of the city near railroad lines and the river, Union Stockyards opened in 1865 and earned for the city the nicknames "Packingtown" and "Hog Butcher to the World."

The Pullman Palace Car Company, providing luxury railroad travel, was located further south at 115th Street. In an effort to "attract good workers and enhance productivity," the company's founder, George M. Pullman, built a town for his workers that would "provide superior living quarters in a healthful setting far from urban problems." But the town did not last long. Within 20 years, bitter labor strikes and lawsuits forced the town's dissolution and Pullman became a part of Chicago.

HOTEL METROPOLE (1891–1994), MICHIGAN AVENUE AND TWENTY-THIRD STREET. Historian Carl Condit argues architect Clinton J. Warren moved from the "sharp-edged regularity" of his Virginia Hotel to curved corners, gently undulating walls, and bay windows when he designed this hotel a year later. Thirty years after the Polter Palmers left the Near South, the white exodus was nearly complete, and this hotel, like others, turned over eventually to African Americans restricted to living in the area.

LEXINGTON HOTEL (1891/1892–1995), NORTHEAST CORNER, MICHIGAN AND TWENTY-SECOND (CERMAK) AVENUES. Following his own Metropole, Clinton J. Warren developed this 10-story building for well-to-do residents and guests attending the 1893 exposition. A 1910 renovation turned it into a popular convention and social headquarters. Moving from the Metropole in 1928, Al Capone lived here until he went to prison in 1931. After becoming a brothel and low-rent residential building, the Metropole closed in 1980.

MECCA HOTEL (1891–1951), 3360 SOUTH STATE STREET. Designed by Daniel Burnham and constructed in time for the 1893 exposition, the Mecca flourished for almost 20 years. As it lost prestige in the second decade of the 20th century, Irish, Italians, and African Americans occupied the building. When the Black Belt developed, Mecca Flats housed mostly African Americans. Many musicians heating up the nearby nightclubs with jazz resided here. (Courtesy of the Chicago History Museum.)

LAKOTA HOTEL (1893–1959), THIRTIETH STREET AND MICHIGAN AVENUE. This elegant building supports some art historians' contention that the architects of the Chicago Style Construction are wrongly understood as being opposed to anything not strictly functional. The sides of this building truly undulate, and the variation of windows from long rectangular ones on the first floor to round peepholes on the final floor are subtle but charming. Note the dome caps on the corners. When compared with the Metropole and Lexington, it is easy to see why some believe Clinton J. Warren is the architect.

(NEW) SOUTHERN HOTEL, MICHIGAN AVENUE AND THIRTEENTH STREET. Establishing lunchrooms caused some hoteliers to fret about the clientele they would draw, but proprietor William C. Keeley was gratified when he opened one in 1915, "A remarkable thing about the patronage is the large number of ladies who wait upon themselves. They seem to like the chair-arm tables and the selection of their own foods, which are displayed in the most appetizing manner, so that each article of food sells itself." (CT, 1911.)

CALVERT HOTEL, 1805 SOUTH WABASH AVENUE. A second-class hotel located "Five Minutes to the Heart of the City" by public transportation, this three-story building includes a corner bay as well as bays interspersed with the flat facade. Living- and guest-quarters were available on the second and third floors, while stores occupied the first. (CT.)

TRANSIT HOUSE (1869–1912), FORTY-FIRST PLACE AND HALSTED STREET. With its cupola and porches, the Transit House looked much like a schoolhouse. Adjacent to the Union Stockyards, it catered to those doing business there—cowboys, drovers, cattlemen, stockmen and purchasing agents. The gate's ornate entrance sign reads "The Unions Stock Yard and Transit Company." The hotel burned in 1912. (VOH, 1912.)

STOCK YARD INN (1912–1976), FORTY-FIRST PLACE AND HALSTED STREET, R. S. LINDSTROM. Built in 1912, the Stock Yard Inn replaced the Transit House. One of the finest examples of Tudor-revival architecture in the country, the inn replicated notable buildings in Great Britain. The hotel was renowned for the Saddle and Sirloin Club and the "beautiful Sirloin Room – where the Steak is born." When the stockyards closed in the 1970s, so did this famous landmark. (A.)

"TONEY'S" HOTEL.

THE DROVERS HOME

4055 S. HALSTED ST.

Opposite Rock Island Division, and only half a block South of the L. S. & M. S. Dummy Track.

MEALS AT ALL HOURS 25c.

LODGING 25c. OYSTERS 25c.

This house is well fitted up for the accommodation of Drovers and Stockmen.

OPEN ALL NIGHT.

D. B. CARMICHAEL, Prop.

"TONEY'S" HOTEL, 4055 SOUTH HALSTED STREET. This hotel for drovers—cattle or sheep herders—was also known as the Drovers Home, as advertised on this trade card—a marketing device in the mid- to late 19th century, later replaced by magazine advertisements and postcards. This hotel offers meals at all hours, indicating the magnitude of the stockyards' operation.

HOTEL FLORENCE (1881–PRESENT), 11111 FORESTVILLE AVENUE. Named after railroad car tycoon George Pullman's daughter, this 125-room hotel opened in the "model" company town of Pullman, 14 miles from the city. The hotel contained a dining room, billiard room, parlor, barbershop, reading-and-meeting room, and the only bar in the town. Pullman kept his own suite of rooms here. Initially off limits to employees, eventually the hotel welcomed workers as guests. The hotel's architect was New Yorker Solon Spencer Beman who also designed the town of Pullman. (CT, 1901.)

Seven

HYDE PARK AND HYDE PARK TOWNSHIP

Little developed this far south of the newly incorporated Chicago until 1853 when Paul Cornell invested in 300 acres to build a town. Naming his village Hyde Park to sell his dream of an elegant suburb over the reality of a swamp, Cornell first divided the land into a simple street grid, deeding 60 acres to the Illinois Central Railroad, assuring transportation into the city. The first hotel, Hyde Park House, opened in 1857, followed a year later by religious congregations, anchoring the emerging community.

After adding a lakefront park, Cornell instigated South Park, a comprehensive park plan by the noted landscape architect Frederick Law Olmsted enclosing Hyde Park on three sides by natural environments—Lake Michigan on the east and two new parks, Jackson Park on the south and Washington Park on the west. The two parks were connected by a narrow strip of land, the Midway Plaisance. The 1892 founding of the University of Chicago completed the final component of Cornell's dream.

In 1889, Chicago annexed Hyde Park township, extending from Thirty-ninth to 138th Streets and from State Street to Lake Michigan. When Chicago won the bid to present the 1893 World's Columbian Exposition, Jackson Park was designated the host venue. Seeing economic opportunity, residents and investors built hotels, rooming houses, saloons, and retail stores.

The fair vastly improved Hyde Park's transportation and solidified commercial niches along the railroad lines. Hotels and resorts continued to prosper while many of the temporary hotels served as rental housing. By the 1900s, this quiet town became a bustling and vibrant neighborhood. For 20 years, as new residents teemed into Hyde Park, row houses and apartments flourished, businesses prospered, and an emerging nightlife took hold.

HYDE PARK HOUSE (1858–1879), FIFTY-THIRD STREET AND THE LAKEFRONT. In 1858, Hyde Park's founder Paul Cornell built the village's first resort hotel on the site of what would become the Sisson Hotel. This four-story wood frame resort with mansard roof was initially built to provide lodging for those exploring the potential homesite or overseeing construction of their new residences. Later, as a resort, it drew the rich and famous to take in the lake breezes and country air. It is said that Albert Edward, Prince of Wales, visited here in 1860 while visiting Chicago. The hotel became home to Mary Todd Lincoln and her sons Robert and Tad, who came to the resort shortly after the president's assassination. The Lincolns remained here for two and a half months before moving downtown to the Clifton House on Wabash Avenue. The Hyde Park House was destroyed by fire in 1879. (Courtesy of the Chicago History Museum.)

HYDE PARK HOTEL (1887–1963), LAKE PARK AVENUE AND HYDE PARK BOULEVARD. Financed by and built on the home site of Hyde Park's founder, Paul Cornell, the exterior design of rounded embayments provided additional space and light in the corner apartments. This design by Theodore Starrett became a standard in many Chicago buildings thereafter. The hotel expanded in 1891 becoming, as guidebooks to the exposition called it, "one of the largest and best furnished hotels in the city." (1910.)

HYDE PARK HOTEL. The hotel expanded again in 1914, doubling its size to 300 and adding on a sun parlor and a 500-seat dining room with skylights of amber glass. During the 1893 fair, room fees ran at first-class prices ($3–$8 per day or $60–$180 in 2004). Eventually the dining room was rented as a cafeteria, and the hotel was divided into kitchenette apartments. (C, 1927.)

Hyde Park Hotel, Lobby. A handsome mosaic floor overlaid with carpets welcomes guests in this 1933 advertising brochure. Formal dress was required for evening meals, and in 1900, the dining rooms "resounded to music every night." An orchestra that "retained its old-time splendor" played in the lobby on Thursdays. Until the hotel's demise, men sat in the lobby at a men's corner.

Bryson Hotel (around the late 1880s until the 1970s), 4932 South Lake Park Avenue. This dual-image card shows both lobby and lounge of this suburban hotel. The dining room is in the background, while a bouquet of flowers dresses the desk in front. The lower card shows the handsome lounge. Serving as a hotel for seniors in the 1960s, it was torn down in the early 1970s, making room for the Kenwood Academy athletic field. (CT.)

GLADSTONE HOTEL (1892–1960S), SIXTY-SECOND STREET AND KENWOOD AVENUE. This postcard describes the property as "A hotel of Cleanliness, Comfort and Courtesy. Residential and Transient. Attractive Rates. European Plan. Café and Cafeteria in Connection." While its architect is unknown, the rounded corners, inset fire escapes, banded cornice and arched windows on the second floor from the top are found also at the Hyde Park Hotel. (LM.)

GLADSTONE HOTEL, LOBBY. The strapwork ceiling, illuminated arches, wainscoting on the stairwell, high-back chairs, and overall English Elizabethan style dominate the lobby of the Gladstone Hotel. Initially built for the 1893 World's Columbian Exposition, the Gladstone continued operations after the fair and provided its guests with fine accommodations through the 1950s. The hotel closed in the early 1960s because of a changed business climate. (CTP, 1915.)

CHICAGO BEACH HOTEL (1890; EXPANSION 1911–LATE 1960S), FIFTY-FIRST STREET AND CORNELL AVENUE. Probably designed by Thomas Starrett and George A. Fuller, the hotel was located five blocks from the 1893 exposition. This six-story brick-and-stone beachfront property was one of Chicago's largest and first resorts serving both residential and transient guests with 450 guest rooms, 175 with baths. Today the site is a collection of mid-rise apartment buildings. (FP, 1915.)

CHICAGO BEACH HOTEL, VIEW FROM NORTH VERANDA. At the porch's furthest end, friends enjoy the view overlooking the lawn and lake affirming the hotel's advertisement, ". . . 400 miles of open water stretches away . . . Whether you seek the restfulness of the country, or more active sports and recreation . . . the quiet efficiency of our service gives each guest a sense of home coming. . .Only ten minutes' ride from the shopping and theater districts." (CT.)

CHICAGO BEACH HOTEL, BATHING BEACH AND PIER. Guests could promenade on the pier or enjoy yachting, canoeing, and bathing. Boardwalks and cabanas were available. The hotel was noted for its family-style and regionally themed dinners such as Creole or New England. This was seen as an innovation and a welcome break from the overbearing and lengthy daily menus. (VOH.)

CHICAGO BEACH HOTEL, VIEW FROM SOUTH VERANDA. The 1,000-foot veranda overlooking the lake and park was "swept by cooling breezes." This, "the Finest Hotel on the Great Lakes," enticed guests with these words: ". . . shaded parks complete the beautiful surroundings. There are walks, drives, sequestered spots and spacious apartments; for the gay there are sailing, bathing, golf, tennis, walking, driving, tally-ho rides, dancing, live music and town amusements. The table is always tempting, and liberally supplied." (VOH, 1910.)

Chicago Beach Hotel, Tennis Courts and Bathing Beach. Although barely visible, the bathing beach is located in the center left of the picture while tennis courts are adjacent to the beach on the east side. This "high class residential, tourist and transient hotel" advertised their 1890 construction and furnished costs at $1 million ($20 million in 2004). (VOH, 1910.)

Chicago Beach Hotel (1911 Expansion). With the 1911 addition, the hotel expanded its activities with indoor and outdoor golf, dancing pavilion, quoits, skating, and moving pictures. During World War II, the hotel became a station hospital for the Army Air Forces Technical Training Command's Chicago Schools and later served as headquarters for the Fifth Army of the United States Armed Forces. Two 36-story luxury apartment towers now occupy the space. (VOH.)

ENGAGE YOUR ROOMS NOW FOR THE WORLD'S FAIR

RATES, $1.00 PER DAY .....AND UPWARDS

SEND FOR PAMPHLET

WE FURNISH THE BEST OF REFERENCES AS TO OUR STANDING

SEND FOR PAMPHLET GIVING FULL PARTICULARS

THE VARSITY HOTEL

(BRICK--NEW--WELL LOCATED)

S. W. COR. ELLIS AVE. AND SIXTY-FIRST ST.

CHICAGO

ELIJAH T. HARRIS
ARTHUR B. CAMP } OWNERS

MARK T. LEONARD, MANAGER

VARSITY HOTEL (BUILT 1893), SOUTHEAST CORNER, ELLIS AVENUE AND SIXTY-FIRST STREET. While many trade cards provided descriptive copy or an image of the product, this card promotes the Varsity Hotel by capturing the imagination of the viewer through the magnificence of the exposition's Transportation Building designed by Louis Sullivan. The Varsity was an eight-story, 250-room brick hotel said to have been tall enough and close enough to the fair that guests could see the Manufacturers and Liberal Arts Building—over a mile away—from the second-floor balcony.

HOTEL HAYES AND ANNEX (1892–1963), SIXTY-FOURTH STREET BETWEEN UNIVERSITY AND WOODLAWN AVENUES. John and Minnie Hayes Sr. built their 120-room hotel in preparation for the 1893 exposition. John Jr. expanded the hotel with its first annex (shown here) to 160 rooms, claiming it to be "Woodlawn's Newest and Only Modern Hotel." The hotel later expanded to 500 rooms.

HOTEL HAYES, NEW LOBBY. This is the earliest of three interior postcards and shows the grand staircase of the hotel on the right, the front office in the middle, and a dark hallway leading back through the hotel. The front office's cashier cage sits to the right of the central column, whose capital seems almost too large for the column itself. The perspective of this illustration is crude and contrasts sharply with the artistic quality of the following two cards. (SE, 1917.)

Hotel Hayes and Annex, Lobby. Both of the postcards on this page are from the same era, after the hotel added a 500-room annex. Here a window seat welcomes guests and transitions them into the old section of the now remodeled hotel. Unfortunately, the front office and grand staircase are not visible in this view. (CT.)

Hotel Hayes and Annex, Lounge. A large fireplace dominates this lounge while chairs, tables, and an occasional sofa scattered throughout lend an informal air. In 1914, the hotel issued an innovative shopping card to permanent guests as "a convenience in their purchasing." The card, according to *Hotel Monthly* "cannot well be used in a transient hotel but for permanents can be done very nicely," acknowledging it was easier to collect tardy payments from full-time residents than overnight guests. (CT.)

HOTEL DEL PRADO (1893–1930), FIFTY-NINTH STREET BETWEEN BLACKSTONE AND KENWOOD STREETS. This double postcard shows the hotel facing the Midway Plaisance—the University of Chicago to the left (west) and the Illinois Central Railroad (center) separates it from Jackson Park. The card shows the recreation it advertises: "two golf courses, tennis courts, lagoons for canoeing, Lake Michigan for bathing, boating, fishing and cruising, equestrian paths, and the finest automobile boulevard in this country." Originally built for the 1893 exposition

HOTEL DEL PRADO. Called the Barry after the fair to honor the brothers who built it, the name changed again in 1895 to Del Prado. Designed by W. D. Cowles, and built as a permanent hotel for the exposition, it later provided accommodations for University of Chicago guests and professors. The hotel was torn down in 1930 to make room for the university's International House. (CRC.)

as the Raymond and Whitcomb Grand, this hotel provided accommodations for those taking part in Raymond's Vacation Excursions, an agency providing tours to the fair and throughout the continent. *Rand McNally* posts the room rate as $10 per day ($200 in 2004). The total tour, at $125 per person, ($2,500) included a week's lodging, 12 fair admissions, and round-trip train service from Philadelphia. (CT.)

HOTEL DEL PRADO, WALK. Taken in sequence with the previous card, this picture of the hotel's front walk shows the veranda extending the full 550 feet of the hotel. Two couples are walking east along the Midway Plaisance towards the lake, perhaps headed for a stroll through Jackson Park. The car on the left is parked in the same spot as the car on the previous page. (CRC, 1908.)

HOTEL DEL PRADO, DINING ROOM. Adjacent to the main lobby, this 9,900-square-foot dining room sat over 500 people. From the lobby, guests also had access to a barbershop, reading rooms, telegraphy office, bazaar, wide staircases, and elevators taking them to their rooms. The hotel also featured the Club—a suite of rooms for meetings decorated in an adventurers' style of the times: dark colors, wood, and hunting trophies. (CTP.)

HARVARD HOTEL, 5714–5720 SOUTH BLACKSTONE AVENUE. Parked in front of this 62-room hotel is what appears to be a Woods Electric motor vehicle produced in Chicago, 1899–1919. This hotel, like so many others built for the fair, fell into disrepair. By the late 1940s and 1950s, it became a notorious criminal hangout. Urban renewal changed the face of, and rescued, Hyde Park. Townhouses now occupy this space. (CRC, 1923.)

Elms Hotel, 1634 East Fifty-third Street. A horseless carriage kicks up a trail of dust as it heads towards the Elms Hotel, conveniently located one block east of the Fifty-third Street train depot. It was "sufferably hot for the past two days" in June, wrote the hotel guest who would be "heading off to Cleveland on Saturday the 27th." Today a two-story retail building occupies the site. (CRC, 1908.)

Holland Hotel, Northwest Corner, Lake Avenue and Fifty-third Street. Located one block west of the same depot as the Elms Hotel, the 400-room Hotel Holland was listed in a guide to the 1893 exposition as a hotel constructed with "everything new and first class." The small building on the left, behind the awning in the foreground, stands today housing a popular neighborhood cafeteria. (CRC.)

VENDOME CLUB HOTEL, SIXTY-SECOND STREET AND MONROE AVENUE (KENWOOD). Guidebooks for the exposition identified the 300-room Vendome as a family hotel built specifically for the fair and charging $2.50 per night, European plan. This brick and stone hotel had a roof garden where refreshments were served. The exterior design is again similar to the Chicago construction of the Hyde Park, Gladstone, and Winamac. The lack of horizontal banding causes the building to soar in height. (CT, 1910.)

VENDOME CLUB HOTEL, RED FOUNTAIN ROOM. In addition to the red fountain (left center), mirrored walls and columns reflecting the decor dominate this colorful dining room. From the ceiling trellis of grape clusters and leaves hang heavily chained, leaded stained-glass chandeliers that provide both the individual tables and the overall space with an additional sense of fantasy.

Vendome Club Hotel, Suite of Sleeping Rooms. A year following the fair, the owners advertised that "comfort, elegance and economy of living" in this hotel "does not belong to that numerous class of temporary structures erected for World's Fair purposes." They also emphasized apartment suites of two, three, and four rooms in addition to the single rooms available for transients. Note the bathtub beyond one of the two rocking chairs and the sink in the bedchamber.

The Waukesha Club, Southeast Corner, Sixty-fourth Street and Washington (Blackstone) Avenue. The Waukesha Club advertised 300 rooms at $2–$5 per night ($40–$100 in 2004) on the European plan. Like so many hotels built for the fair, the Waukesha Club became apartments, fell into disrepair, and was razed. The Wadsworth Child-Care Education Center occupies the site. (FAN.)

WINDERMERE HOTEL (1893–1959), NORTHWEST CORNER, FIFTY-SIXTH STREET AND CORNELL AVENUE. The Windermere was built across from Esquimaux Village, the Texas building, and an entrance to the exposition. Although designed for fairgoers, the 250-room hotel was a permanent structure and remained operating through the 1950s. Identified as "one of the country's great luxury hotels," the Windermere boasted it was the first hotel to provide telephones in every room—a similar claim of New York's Waldorf and Chicago's Palmer House. (CT.)

WINDERMERE HOTEL, GARDEN. This formal garden between the hotel (unseen) and the ivy-covered building provided formal outdoor spaces walled with trailing vines and a fountain for refreshment. Nearby, the hotel added on a long and narrow tropical sunroom, called the "Palm Room," that was furnished by Marshall Field and Company. Today, the site of the garden and the Windermere West is a parking lot and the Bret Harte Elementary School. (CT.)

WINDERMERE HOTEL. By 1911, the hotel expanded, marketed itself as a "high class residential hotel" that was "better than when new," and added an elongated veranda mirroring the resort-like feel of Chicago Beach and Del Prado. This card emphasizes the hotel's park-like setting and features a couple strolling through Jackson Park, perhaps on their way to the Field Columbian Museum, now the Museum of Science and Industry. (1911.)

HOTELS WINDERMERE (1893–1959 AND 1922/1923–PRESENT), EAST: 1642 EAST FIFTY-SIXTH STREET. The contrast between the old construction and the Rapp and Rapp's Beaux Arts building with 450 guest rooms and 250 apartments is apparent. The front entrance, an elaborate porte cocheres, is a hallmark of this style apartment hotel. Guests included architect Louis Sullivan, financier John Rockefeller, and writers Edna Ferber, Phillip Roth, and Thomas Mann. It was listed in the National Register of Historic Places in 1982. (CT, 1927.)

Colonial Hotel, Sixty-third Street and Kenwood Avenue. A tree-lined street with benches along the sidewalk augments the welcoming feel of this four-story, 150-room hotel with veranda and pink awnings. An 1893 exposition guide indicates the Colonial was built specifically for the fair but fails to list room charges. Still operating for the second world's fair hosted by Chicago, the 1933 A Century of Progress, the reverse of this card advertises "Colonial Hospitality." (CT.)

Winamac, 830 Oakwood Boulevard. Bay windows and rounded corners reflect the essential features of Chicago construction. Heavy horizontal lines, strong cornice, and a light-stone first floor contribute to the stacked look of this six-story building. Besides single people and couples, the Winamac states that "groups of three, four, or five are welcomed." (CT.)

DREXEL VIEW HOTEL, DREXEL BOULEVARD AT FORTY-FOURTH STREET. Overlooking Chicago's most beautiful boulevard, the Drexel View Hotel was "a residential hotel for particular people at moderate rates." The hotel provided full dining and room services. Today Martin Luther King Jr. High School is located here.

DREXEL ARMS HOTEL, DREXEL AND OAKWOOD BOULEVARDS. The Drexel Hotel reemerged as Drexel Arms after a renovation in 1906 that included a new addition doubling the size of the hotel. *Hotel Monthly* reported that the "ground floor is used for office, lobby, ladies sitting room, dining room, café and kitchen . . . The telephones are in the halls and guests . . can . . . pay by dropping coins into the slot." (CC, 1933.)

THE SISSON HOTEL (1917–PRESENT), 5300 SOUTH SHORE DRIVE. Built on the site of the Hyde Park House, this hotel has a sordid past. In 1923, the American Unity League's allegation that proprietor Harry W. Sisson was a member of the Ku Klux Klan resulted in Jews and Catholics boycotting the hotel. As a counteraction, Klansmen were urged to stay at the hotel. By the height of the Big Band era, things had changed. Renamed Hotel Sherry, Duke Ellington performed here, and Jewish weddings were conducted in the ballroom. (MRS.)

THE ELSTON, 4173 SOUTH LAKE PARK AVENUE. Resembling both the Vendome and the early Chicago Beach, this second-class hotel proudly advertised its "Nice, Clean Outside Kitchenettes and Sleeping Rooms with running water." As a self-identified "tourists headquarters," the Elston offered to make arrangements for couples and groups. (1933.)

Cooper-Carlton Hotel (1918–Present), Hyde Park Boulevard at Fifty-third Street. Promoting a resort-like setting, this postcard fails to include the nearby Sisson, misleading viewers to believe the Cooper-Carlton stood alone. The hotel boasts ". . . every advantage of the best downtown hotels, plus good air, quiet and pleasant environments of the park and lake." Renamed the Del Prado, after the original Del Prado was torn down in 1930, the structure today is a 198-unit rental apartment building. (C.)

Manor House Hotel, 4635 South Parkway (Martin Luther King Drive). This Queen Anne–style building was probably built in the late 19th century as a single-family home and became a single-room occupancy hotel as the neighborhood changed from wealthy to disadvantaged—a common fate for these glorious buildings. Today they are highly prized and are being restored to their original elegance. (CT.)

THE WEDGEWOOD, WOODLAWN AVENUE AT SIXTY-FOURTH STREET. Because of its narrow triangular form, the building is described as a flatiron, the shape of an old-fashioned clothes iron. Located near an elevated line and Illinois Central depot, the hotel was popular with visitors to the local parks and beaches. The hotel and neighborhood fell into disrepair in the 1950s. The building is gone, but the land retains the flatiron shape. (CT.)

HOTEL STRAND, SIXTY-THIRD STREET AND COTTAGE GROVE AVENUE. A segment of a letter from a hotel guest to her "Dear Friend Ada" marks a new era: "So you have 'gone and done it.' I had been wondering for a long time if you had the necessary courage to have your hair bobbed. They are all doing it out here so you are undoubtedly right in style."

Eight

A Look at the 1920s

Immediately after World War I, a population and building boom began that would have a profound effect on Chicago and its hotels. The city's population jumped from over 1.5 million in 1900 to 3.3 million by the end of the 1920s. New train stations, an airport, bridges, roads, and office buildings were constructed. Prohibition and gangsters showed the dark side of the city, while jazz and entertainment remained in the bright light. The 1920s was the age of the grand palace hotels that took luxury, even if a facade, and claimed it for their own. Opulent public spaces like ballrooms, lobbies, show rooms for orchestras, ice skating, and supper clubs with famous celebrities all underscored the hotels' magic.

This decade of a growing economy saw the emergence of the convention hotel because of demand for more meeting space and services by corporations and associations for their expanding events. Hotels responded with more and larger meeting rooms, exhibition halls, and public stenographers' offices. Municipal (Navy) Pier joined the Coliseum as an exhibit hall requiring hotels to provide more guest rooms.

The decade of the 1920s was also the golden age of apartment hotels—welcoming both residential and transient guests. Apartment hotels took on a life of their own as those who could afford it made their full-time residence in a building with multiple suites and all of the services of a regular hotel, dining room service, maid service, and laundry.

All were represented in Chicago. Two styles symbolizing the era are included here: the small hotel and the grand palace.

THE PEARSON (1923–1971), 190 EAST PEARSON STREET. The neoclassical residential and transient Pearson, designed by Robert S. DeGolyer, was located in the heart of the near the north side apartment and hotel district, serving those travelers who sought a quieter stay in Chicago. The Ritz-Carlton occupies the site today. (CT.)

THE DRAKE (1920–PRESENT), 140 EAST WALTON PLACE. The Drake's first owners were brothers John B. and Tracy Drake, also owners and managers of the Blackstone. With the city's most prominent hotels at either end of Michigan Avenue (both designed by Marshall and Fox), it seemed as though the Drakes encompassed the social, commercial, and political life of Chicago. As one of the grandest of Chicago's palace hotels, the Drake continues to play host to dignitaries, celebrities, and citizens alike.

SOVEREIGN HOTEL, (1922–PRESENT), NORTHEAST CORNER, GRANVILLE AND KENMORE AVENUES. With 600 guest rooms, two ballrooms, and a swimming pool, the Sovereign was a major factor in the urbanization of the North Edgewater area. Ten stories high and noted for its elegant terra cotta cornice, the hotel by West Ahlschlager is a fine example of the Beaux Arts style. The building is now apartments and home to the Edgewater Athletic Center.

SOVEREIGN HOTEL, MAIN ENTRANCE HALL. Among the hotel's guests were Charlie Chaplin, the Duke of Windsor, the King of Denmark, Al Capone, and the Andrew Sisters. In his youth, Johnny Weismmuller, star of the epic film *Tarzan* and Olympic swim team member in 1924 and 1928, was a lifeguard at the hotel's pool. He practiced at a similar pool at the Medina Club, now the Hotel Intercontinental on North Michigan Avenue.

SHORELAND (1925–PRESENT), 5454 SOUTH SHORE DRIVE. With sports facilities, grand and crystal ballrooms, a Louis XVI dining room, and a castilian grill room, the 1,000-room Shoreland Hotel, designed by Friedstein and Company, became a center of Hyde Park's social life. The inaccurately pictured lakefront displays a hoped-for vision. Current plans call for the building, a University of Chicago dormitory, to be converted into condominiums. (CT.)

SHORELAND, MAIN LOBBY. The soaring ceiling supported by squared Corinthian columns, magnificent chandeliers, palms, and bamboo furniture created a tropical fantasy in this lobby. As modernity set in, the décor changed from exotic to art deco. The Shoreland played host to baseball teams in town to play the White Sox and attracted celebrities including Amelia Earhart, Al Capone, Elvis Presley, and Jimmy Hoffa. The hotel served as a temporary hospital for soldiers of World War II. (ECK.)

THE STEVENS (1927–PRESENT), 720 SOUTH MICHIGAN AVENUE. With a children's playroom, 1200-seat theater, 18-hole rooftop miniature golf course, ice-cream factory, electric power plant, hospital, and 3,000 rooms, architects Holabird and Roche created the world's largest hotel in 1927. Purchased and named after Conrad Hilton in the late 1940s, the hotel was completely renovated in 1984–1985. For its 75th anniversary in 2002, it was renamed Hilton Chicago.

THE STEVENS, THE GRAND STAIR HALL. The Stevens' imposing and inspiring grand stair hall transports guests to regal splendor. At the top, guests move to the main dining room, writing room, or grand banquet hall. Marble colonnades line both sides of the second story. A fresco adorns the ceiling, and bronze and crystal chandeliers illuminate the space. The Stevens exemplifies the meaning of grand palace hotel.

Image Sources

The publisher of each postcard, when available, is indicated by the following abbreviations. These abbreviations conform to those developed by Leslie Hudson in her Arcadia titles. The postmark date, when available, is indicated.

Code	Publisher
A	The Acmegraph Company, Chicago
AC	American Colortype
AH	A. Holzman, Chicago and Leipzig
C	Commercialchrome
CC	Commercial Colortype
CCC	The Caregill Company
CRC	C. R. Childs, Chicago
CT	Curt Teich and Company, Chicago also Curteich
CTP	CT Photochrome, by Curt Teich and Company
DP	Detroit Publishing Company
EA	Empire Art Company, Chicago
ECK	E. C. Kropp Company, Milwaukee
FAN	F. A. Naber Publishing
FP	Franklin Post Card Company, Chicago
GB	Gerson Brothers, Chicago
HGZ	H. G. Zimmerman and Company, Chicago
IT	Isler—Tompsett, Saint Louis
LM	Leon Morgan Publisher, Chicago
ML	Michigan Litho
MRS	Max Rigot Selling Company, Chicago
NYP	New York Postal Card Company, Chicago
SE	Sexichrome
SH	Sherwood Litho
SU	Suhling and Koehn Company Publishing, Chicago
VOH	V. O. Hammon Publishing Company, Chicago
WN	Western News Company
WPL	Western P and L

Bibliography

Block, Jean. F. *Hyde Park Houses: An Informal History, 1856–1910.* Chicago and London: The University of Chicago Press, 1978.
Condit, Carl W. *The Chicago School of Architecture.* Chicago and London: The University of Chicago Press, 1964.
Holt, Glen E. and Dominic A. Pacyga. *Chicago: A Guide to the Neighborhoods – The Loop and the South Side.* Chicago: Chicago Historical Society, 1979.
Mayer, Harold, M. and Richard C. Wade. *Chicago: Growth of a Metropolis.* Chicago and London: The University of Chicago Press, 1969.
Morely, John. *The History of Furniture: Twenty-five Centuries of Style and Design in the Western Tradition.* London: Bulfinch Press, 1999.
Randal, Frank. *History of the Development of Building Construction in Chicago.* Second Edition. A. John D. Randall (rev. and expanded). Urbana and Chicago: University of Illinois Press, 1999.
Sinkevitvch, Alice, ed. *AIA Guide to Chicago, 2nd Edition.* Orlando: Harcourt, Inc. 2004.
Waldheim, Charles and Katerina Rüedi Ray (eds.), *Chicago Architecture: Histories, Revisions, Alternatives.* Chicago and London: University of Chicago Press, 2005.
Zukowsky, John. (ed.), *Chicago Architecture 1871–1922: Birth of a Metropolis.* Munich, London, New York: Prestel, 1987 first edition, reprinted 1988, 2000.

INDEX